Haunted
West Virginia

Haunted West Virginia

Ghosts & Strange Phenomena
of the Mountain State

Patty A. Wilson

Illustrations by Heather Adel Wiggins

STACKPOLE
BOOKS

To my friend Jenifer Roberts,
who introduced me to West Virginia's ghostly side.

To my children, who are always my inspiration—
including Jenna, who has become part of our family.

And to all of those who have had paranormal experiences
and shared their tales with others.

Copyright © 2007 by Patty A. Wilson

Published by
STACKPOLE BOOKS
5067 Ritter Road
Mechanicsburg, PA 17055
www.stackpolebooks.com

Printed in the United States of America

10 9 8 7 6

FIRST EDITION

Design by Beth Oberholtzer
Cover design by Caroline Stover

Library of Congress Cataloging-in-Publication Data

Wilson, Patty A.
    Haunted West Virginia : ghosts and strange phenomena of the mountain state / Patty A. Wilson.–1st ed.
        p.   cm.
    Includes bibliographical references.
    ISBN-13: 978-0-8117-3400-4 (pbk.)
    ISBN-10: 0-8117-3400-5 (pbk.)
    1. Ghosts–West Virginia. 2. Monsters–West Virginia. 3. Haunted places–West Virginia. I. Title.
BF1472.U6W558   2007
133.109754–dc22

2007000347

Contents

Introduction

AT THE BEGINNING OF THE TWENTY-FIRST CENTURY, ABOUT HALF OF ALL
Americans believe in ghosts. Ghosts are thought to haunt for many
reasons. They may be reliving important past moments, righting
wrongs, or fulfilling promises. It often seems that a great passion,
love, or turmoil drives the dead to reach back into this world to
influence the living.

West Virginia was birthed by the passions that churned during
the Civil War. The people of Virginia split over the issue of seceding
from the United States at the beginning of the war. The people of
the western part of Virginia were patriotic and chose to leave their
mother state rather than abandon the great experiment of liberty
that was the United States. But that decision also caused great turmoil for the people of the land now called West Virginia.

As a historian, I have come to realize that a region's ghost stories represent the history of a people and reflect their culture,
beliefs, and hopes. I have been honored to get to know the people
of West Virginia so well and am impressed by their bravery,
endurance, and hard work. The people of the Mountain State are
proud, independent, and tough, and their stories are as diverse and
colorful as they are.

Some of the stories in this book are oft told because they are an
enduring part of the fabric of the people of West Virginia. Others
have never been told publicly before. I hope you enjoy reading the
unusual tales of hauntings and other mysterious phenomena set in
this rugged state.

New River and Greenbrier Valleys

The Headless Man of Fayette County

When the railroads arrived in the area, they changed more than the topography. People found the flat, level railroad beds easy to walk. The railroads were the most direct route between towns, and because of the convenience, people often ignored the danger of walking along the tracks. As they walked along, they frequently met others traveling the same route, and they would pass a pleasant hour or two until they reached their destination.

From time to time there were tragic accidents. On occasion, a traveler made a grisly discovery, finding a decapitated body or one that was cut in half. Train engineers often didn't realize they had struck someone and did not stop. Many stories are told of railroad tracks where pedestrians or railroad workers haunt the scene of their death.

People walking along the tracks between the towns of Pax and Weirwood in Fayette County have reported seeing bright lights dancing erratically in the distance ahead of them. Somehow the lights manage to keep the same distance between them and whoever is watching them, no matter how hard people try to catch up to them.

When people reach the bridge between Pax and Weirwood, they see the lights suddenly come together to form the glowing image of a headless man. Horrified, they watch as the figure stumbles along toward the bridge. Suddenly the man is gone, and the poor witnesses look around in terror, realizing they are all alone on the deserted railroad tracks after just having witnessed the apparition of a headless man. As they glance around, they realize that the headless man has somehow gotten behind them.

The headless man stumbles toward them, and they are forced to step onto the bridge to avoid being touched by the repellent figure. As the witnesses watch, the phantom plunges off the bridge into the water. Only later do these people learn that their experience is not unique. They have encountered the ghost lights of Fayette County.

As local legend has it, a man was walking along the tracks when he was taken by surprise by a train running quickly toward him. The man either stumbled or tried to lie down on the track, but he wound up being beheaded. His body plunged into the river below the railroad bridge, and his head was never found. It is said that on occasion the man returns to search for his head. He relives the last few seconds of his life, but he never finds his head. Until he does, the headless man will never rest.

The Mean-Spirited Spirit

"Come to America, young man, the streets are paved with gold," or so people said in Europe in the 1920s. Europe was experiencing an economic depression, and people all over the continent were suffering. Europeans heard from relatives and friends who had gone before them that across the ocean lay a land of riches and opportunity, and many thought about making the journey to America in search of a better life. Mr. Jachimowicz was one of them. He decided that he and his family would make the journey from Poland so that his five children could grow up in the land of opportunity. They poured every cent they had into the journey.

Unfortunately, the Jachimowicz family did not find a rich, new life in America. Though Mr. Jachimowicz had been a respected scholar and teacher in Poland, his education was not recognized in America, and he could not teach. Instead, he was forced to take a job in the dangerous coal mines of Fayette County, West Virginia, in order to feed his family. The mine owners had company housing on Wingrove Hill for mine families, and the Jachimowiczes moved into one of those little houses.

Soon the family across the street came over to introduce themselves. The Dudas were also immigrants who had come to work in the coal mines, and their children were similar in age to the Jachimowicz youngsters. It was not long until the two families were very close. They visited back and forth, and Mrs. Jachimowicz and Mrs. Duda became friends.

One day Mrs. Duda confided that her family had a secret: They were living in a haunted house, and the spirit there was a mean prankster who did terrible things. She told Mrs. Jachimowicz stories of events in the house, telling her the spirit could speak out loud for anyone to hear and that he mocked them, threw things at them, and made life miserable.

Mrs. Jachimowicz believed that ghosts were possible, but she did not have any direct experience in dealing with them. Still, Mrs. Duda was her friend, and she was determined to support her.

One day Mrs. Jachimowicz's sister was visiting, when there was a frantic pounding at the door. Mrs. Jachimowicz hurried to open it, to see a very distraught Mrs. Duda. The poor woman was terrified. She insisted that the ghost was sewing spectral cloth on her treadle sewing machine and begged the two women to accompany her back to her house.

The three women rushed to the Duda house, and the sisters were shocked to see the sewing machine pumping away without anyone visible working it. On it was a white sheer cloth that was gauzy, almost misty in nature. As the women watched, the cloth was suddenly pulled out from under the needle and whisked up into the air, where it promptly disappeared. The treadle on the sewing machine slowed down and then drew to a halt. Who or what had used the treadle machine would forever remain a mystery.

On another occasion, Mrs. Duda asked Mrs. Jachimowicz to help her change a lightbulb in the downstairs closet under the stairs, as she was too short to reach the bulb. Mrs. Jachimowicz was a good bit taller and was glad to help her friend out. She stepped into the closet and reached up to unscrew the burned-out bulb, when the closet door suddenly slammed shut. Shocked and more than a bit unnerved by the turn of events, Mrs. Jachimowicz grasped the door handle and twisted. Nothing happened. She shouldered into the door, but again it held. She pounded on the door and called out for help. Outside the closet, she could hear Mrs. Duda as she desperately tried to get in to help her friend. Mrs. Jachimowicz tried to calm down. The door was simply locked, she thought. She needed to calm down her friend and find out how to unlock it.

"The door's locked," she called out. "How do we unlock it?" She was trying to be rational, but being locked in a closet in a haunted house did not make that easy.

"It can't be locked," Mrs. Duda said. "It doesn't have a lock."

Mrs. Jachimowicz felt around the doorknob and realized that her friend was right.

Despite their best efforts, the door would not budge. Hours passed, and Mrs. Jachimowicz was increasingly hot, tired, and frightened. She knew she'd have to wait until her husband came home to get help. Somehow he would get her out of the closet. But suddenly the door swung itself open, to the relief of both women. As Mrs. Jachimowicz scurried from the closet, the "burned-out" lightbulb winked on. Both women were left to wonder whether the ghost had set a trap to amuse himself by frightening someone.

Early one morning, Mr. Duda asked his neighbor for help lifting a heavy cast-iron cookstove from the backyard into the kitchen and hooking it up. Mr. Jachimowicz was happy to help his neighbor, but lifting the cookstove would be quite a job for two men. Furthermore, he was curious about why Mr. Duda would be hooking up a cookstove so early in the morning, when they both had to get to work.

Mr. Duda confided that he had not bought a new stove, but had to rehook his old one. The night before, he and family had been sitting at the kitchen table before dinner, waiting for biscuits in the oven to finish. The biscuits only had a couple minutes to go, so they began to fill their plates. Suddenly the door of the oven slammed open, and the hot biscuits began to fling themselves out of the oven at the family. They ran so that the hot projectile biscuits would not hit them. Soon the rain of biscuits was over, and the family merely picked them up, cleaned up the mess, and began to eat supper. Bizarre occurrences were an almost daily event, and the family was no longer shocked by such foolishness as flying biscuits.

The next morning Mrs. Duda had gotten up to start the fire in the stove and begin breakfast, when she discovered that the stove was gone. She called for her husband, and they both thought they had been robbed, until Mr. Duda chanced to see the stove sitting in the backyard in the early morning light. That was why he needed to get it hooked up before work. The ghost had unhooked it and carried it outside in the middle of the night!

For more than a month, the Duda family withstood the pranks, the mean-spirited jokes, and the nasty ghost's attitude, but at last an event happened that made them flee the house.

Mrs. Duda later explained to Mrs. Jachimowicz that one night the family had been sleeping when the most terrifying event occurred. Each person had been awakened in the middle of the night by the feeling of being pinned down in bed. Then their beds were lifted and floated out of the house while they were helpless to get up. The beds were tossed unceremoniously into the front yard, where the family found themselves in a tangle of bedclothes and mattresses. That was enough. If the message was for the family to get out, then get out they would. They quickly moved.

The Jachimowiczes were sorry to see their friends go, but they were glad the family would find some peace, and they hoped the ghost would not bother the next family to move in. They were not prepared for what was about to happen.

While the house across the street sat empty, one night there was a pounding on the door of the Jachimowicz home. Mr. Jachimowicz answered it but found that no one was there. He shut the door just as a deep male voice began laughing. Quickly he snatched open the door again, but no one was there. Still the laughing continued. The frightened family knew immediately that the ghost of the Duda house had come calling. Apparently he was lonely and needed someone to haunt.

For weeks, the family was treated to a display of the specter's nasty humor. Night after night, it pounded on the door and laughed or mocked them. One night Mr. Jachimowicz opened the door in disgust and shouted, "Go back where you came from!" With that, the evil male laughter suddenly entered the house for the first time. It seemed to float over the heads of each family member in the living room while it laughed at them. After that, the spirit came and went as it pleased.

One day Mrs. Jachimowicz tripped over her daughter Helena's shoes while working in the kitchen. She called out in Polish,

"Helena, come here!" Suddenly a voice mocked Mrs. Jachimowicz: "Helena, come here!" Mrs. Jachimowicz swung around expecting to confront Helena, whom she thought was teasing her. But then she realized that it was the spirit, and she cursed it in her native tongue. The spirit seemed to think it was funny. "Dee-dah Hockey . . ." it shouted gleefully over and over. Mrs. Jachimowicz realized that it was poking fun at the names Duda and Jachimowicz, which in English sounded like "Yockey."

The spirit continued to torment the family for weeks. It often made sounds like someone chopping wood outside all night long, but in the morning, there was no wood chopped and nothing was moved.

Eventually another family moved into the former Duda house, and the spirit suddenly stopped visiting the Jachimowiczes. Time after time, folks moved into the house, only to move out a few weeks later. Some confessed that the house was haunted; others refused to say a word. Each time the house was vacant, the Jachimowicz family was subjected to the haunting until new occupants arrived.

Eventually Mrs. Jachimowicz found out who might be haunting the house. A neighbor woman mentioned to her that an old man had hanged himself in the closet on the first floor of the house in the entry hall a few years earlier. Mrs. Jachimowicz remembered that closet well. She believed that the old man who had committed suicide was haunting the house, and that he made fun of the immigrant people because of their languages and their different ways.

Eventually no one would live in the house, and it sat empty for a long time. In the early 1980s, the house caught fire and burned down. No one was sorry to see the old eyesore go. Yet for the descendants of the Jachimowicz family, the house and the grounds held a special significance. They had all grown up hearing the stories of the house and the strange haunting that had plagued their family.

The Ghost Who Solved Her Own Murder

In all of American judicial history, there are only a few cases where spirits are mentioned. Of these, one account stands out, because the ghost solved her own murder, and her words were entered as testimony in a court of law.

Miss Elva Zona Heaster married Erasmus Shue at the local Methodist church in Livesay's Mills in November 1896. Although the bride and groom were quite happy, Zona's mother was worried. She was not sure that she approved of her new son-in-law. The young man had come from the town of White Sulphur Springs to work in the local blacksmith's shop. He appeared to hold down a steady job, but there were rumors about him that worried Zona's mother. She had heard that he was a womanizer, that he gambled, and that he kept unsavory company. Even more sinister stories circulated around the town about his past, and gossips claimed that not only had Erasmus Shue been married twice before, but he had buried both of his young wives under mysterious circumstances. But to speak against the young man only would have made Zona defend him all the more, so Mrs. Heaster was left to worry silently about her daughter's safety.

Zona was a pretty young woman who came from a good family, and she could have married any of the young men in town, but the glib young blacksmith had swept her off her feet. She was head over heels in love with the dark-haired young man. But within weeks of marrying Erasmus Shue, she seemed to have lost her joy. Her mother watched sadly as Zona grew quiet and pale. Dark circles appeared beneath her eyes, and mysterious bruises branded her flesh. Suddenly the graceful young woman became accident-prone. Strange, ugly bruises marred her pale cheeks, and often Zona winced when hugged because her ribs were bruised or broken. There was no question that Erasmus Shue was a terrible husband who beat his young bride savagely. But the more she was questioned, the more Zona lied to protect her husband. She made excuses and refused to discuss the topic of her husband's conduct when her mother brought it up.

Mrs. Heaster feared for her daughter's safety. She wished she could take her child away from the brutal man whom she now had to call a son.

In January 1897, less than three months after the young couple had wed, Zona fell ill. For weeks the doctor tended to Zona, but he could not diagnose her illness. Throughout it all, Erasmus was the very picture of concern. He paid the doctor, left Zona's side only to go to work, and made a show of how worried he was about his wife. On the morning of January 22, Erasmus went to the cabin of a local African American woman known as "Aunt" Martha Jones to ask if her son Anderson could go to the house to do some chores for his wife the next day. Mrs. Jones said that Anderson could do the chores in the afternoon, but that he had promised the doctor he would help him all morning long. Shue was insistent that the twelve-year-old boy be at his house no later than early afternoon.

When the young boy arrived at the Shue house, no one answered the door. He was aware that Zona had been ill, and he had been instructed by Erasmus Shue to go on in if no one answered the door. Young Anderson pushed open the kitchen door and entered the house. He called out for Mrs. Shue, but there was no answer. The boy walked through the house and found Mrs. Shue's body in the dining room. She lay either unconscious or dead on the floor.

Terrified, the young boy ran to the blacksmith shop to tell Erasmus what had happened to his wife. The physician, Dr. Knapp, was summoned, and when he got to the house, Zona's body was lying on her bed in the master bedroom. Erasmus Shue was cradling her head and shoulders and sobbing over her. Oddly, Erasmus had placed a stiff, high collar around the dead woman's neck and wrapped a scarf around the collar in order to hold it in place. When Dr. Knapp approached the woman to see if she were alive, Shue refused to let go of his wife. He held tenaciously to her shoulders and head, and the doctor could not get near her neck to check for vital signs. The doctor assumed that Shue was wracked by grief and did not force the issue of touching Zona's neck, because he could not find a pulse at her wrist and believed her to be dead.

Zona's body was laid out to rest at her mother's home, but her husband still would not leave her side for a moment. People remarked upon how dedicated he was and how horrible his grief must be that he would never leave the head of the coffin. Erasmus insisted on dressing Zona for the funeral himself. He also insisted that she wear a scarf wrapped around her neck, saying she had admired that fashion. No one had ever seen her wear such a fashion before, but who would argue with the grieving husband?

Throughout the entire proceeding, Mrs. Heaster had her suspicions about her daughter's death, and she voiced her opinions loudly. It was soon obvious that Erasmus and Mrs. Heaster did not like each other. The grieving woman told everyone about the beatings her daughter had taken, but Erasmus denied it vehemently. He said that Zona had fallen quite often because she was ill, and all he had ever done was to love her and try to protect her.

The official cause of death of Zona Heaster Shue was death by natural causes, and her physician listed heart failure on the death certificate. Another local doctor also floated the idea of a mysterious hysterical pregnancy. None of this made sense to Mrs. Heaster, who had kissed a healthy young woman good-bye on her wedding day less than three months earlier.

According to Mrs. Heaster, a bizarre event occurred that she believed was a sign from her daughter that the death had not been natural. Mrs. Heaster spoke to her son-in-law only days after the funeral and tried to return to him some sheets that he had used to cover Zona's body, but Shue refused to take the sheets back. Mrs. Heaster decided that she would wash the sheets and lay them away to return to him later. When she washed them, she was surprised to see the water turn pink around the white sheets, and then the sheets began to take on a pink color. Suddenly the pink water turned clear again, but the sheets remained stained. Mrs. Heaster stared at the sheets and felt a sudden conviction that this was sign from her daughter that something was terribly wrong about her death. After that, Mrs. Heaster began to worry incessantly that her daughter had been murdered. She expressed her concerns to family and friends but tried to force her terrible fears aside because there was no evidence of foul play.

Mrs. Heaster begged God to help her find the real reason for her daughter's death. She did not believe the doctors or her son-in-law. She felt that her daughter had been murdered. She would later testify that one night she was in prayer in her bedroom when she looked up and saw her daughter standing in a corner of the room. Zona wore the dress that she had been found dead in. When her mother stood up to go to her, Zona faded away. But the next night, she returned to her mother's bedroom and told her she had been beaten and strangled by her husband during a heated argument they had because she had not cooked meat for supper the night before. Altogether, Zona came to her mother four times before completing her terrible story.

Armed with the knowledge of what had really happened to her daughter, Mrs. Heaster contacted the prosecuting attorney, John A. Preston. When Preston sat down to listen to the woman's story, he was a skeptic, but by the time she had finished speaking, he believed her. Preston called in Dr. Knapp, who had signed Zona's death certificate, and questioned him arduously about his findings. The doctor finally admitted that the verdict of heart failure was not accurate. Then Preston promised Mrs. Heaster that he would exhume her daughter's body and have a proper autopsy done so that she would no longer have any questions about the cause of death.

An exhumation order was filed, and Zona's body was exhumed. Preston's actions in exhuming the body of the young woman were not widely accepted. In fact, some of the staff at the cemetery refused to cooperate until they were threatened with arrest. The body was brought back to the original attending physician, who had given the wrong cause of death, and he was ordered to give Mrs. Heaster an honest answer about how her daughter had died.

The autopsy was performed in the Nickell School House, near the Soule Methodist cemetery where Zona had been buried. The children had been sent home for the day, and kerosene lamps were lit so that Dr. Knapp could perform the autopsy. Erasmus Shue protested loudly about the autopsy and said he knew it would lead to his arrest. "But they will not be able to prove I did it," he said. His comments indicated to the police and prosecuting attorney that he had knowledge of what they would find.

Three hours went by before Dr. Knapp admitted that Zona Shue had been murdered by strangulation. Later a local gossip claimed that the doctor had been a friend of Shue's and had attempted to protect his friend from murder charges. That, however, remained unproven.

On June 30, 1897, Erasmus Shue stood trial for the murder of his wife in the city of Lewisburg. His supporters obtained the services of two prominent attorneys to defend him. By no means would it be easy to get a conviction. The original death certificate had stated heart failure as the cause of death, and that would not be easy to get around. The attorneys would argue that Zona was strangled after she had expired. They even attempted to point the finger of blame at young Anderson Jones.

The prosecuting attorney faced an uphill battle. He did not want the ghost story to come out and instructed Mrs. Heaster to stick with the facts. He wanted her to appear sane and rational at all times. Mrs. Heaster was only to testify that she was the first to notice her

son-in-law's suspicious behavior, and that she had witnessed some oddities about her daughter's body. She was to testify that her daughter's head was extremely "loose," and that Shue had placed a pillow on one side of Zona's head in the coffin and a rolled-up piece of cloth on the other side. When asked why he had done this, Shue had given an unreasonable answer: "to make her comfortable."

The defense attorney, however, decided to bring up the ghost story to make Mrs. Heaster look irrational and superstitious. Unfortunately for him, it did not serve that purpose. Mrs. Heaster stuck to her story about Zona's visitations despite the defense attorney's rude characterizations and insinuations that she had been hallucinating. But Mrs. Heaster never changed her story. In fact, his treatment of the woman and her dogged honesty undermined the defense. He looked like a heartless bully picking on the poor grieving mother.

Zona's mother stated for the record that Zona had appeared in her mother's bedroom four times. Mrs. Heaster testified that Zona told her she had been killed because her husband had been furious that she had not cooked any meat for supper the night before. Zona told her mother that he had "squeezed her neck off at the first joint." Zona's mother also testified that as her daughter had departed on one of her visits, she turned her entire head around at the neck as if to prove her point that her neck was indeed broken. Mrs. Heaster did not believe that she had seen the ghost of her daughter. Rather, she thought her daughter had returned in the flesh to seek justice. She testified that when she touched her daughter, she felt solid and real.

Anderson Jones was called to testify that Shue had been insistent that the boy go to the house alone. The prosecuting attorney stated that Shue wanted to make sure someone else found the body, so he had set up the situation so that the little boy would find his dead wife.

The defense argued that a roving vagabond might have entered the house and found the sick woman alone and killed her. They attempted to state that the motive might have been robbery. But no one had mentioned that anything had been missing from the Shue house, and neighbors were brought in to testify that no strangers were about in the neighborhood on the morning of Zona's murder.

During the trial, information about the supposed accidental deaths of Shue's first two wives also became news. But his first wife, Allie Estelline Cutlip, was located alive, although until her appearance in court, she had been thought dead. She stated that she had married Shue in 1886, and they had lived in a cabin in Rock Camp Run in Pocahontas County, West Virginia. He had beaten her badly several times, so she had taken their child and left him while he was in the penitentiary for stealing a horse. She sued for divorce soon afterward and was granted one based on the violence that had been perpetrated against her.

The second Mrs. Shue, Lucy Ann Tritt, had lived with her husband on Droop Mountain for less than eight months before she died under suspicious circumstances. Lucy was said to have fallen and struck her head on a rock, but many of those who knew her did not believe Shue, although he was never charged with any crime in connection with her death.

Shue had exhibited strange behavior ever since Zona's body had been discovered. He had been alternately madly happy and horribly depressed, playing the grieving husband. He was found guilty of the murder of Zona Shue and was sentenced to life in prison, where he continued his strange behavior. At one point he announced that he was done grieving for his wife, and that when he was released from jail he would find a new wife. He told inmates and the jail staff that he had always planned to marry seven times, and that since he was still a young man, he had a good chance of accomplishing it. He granted interviews to reporters and bragged that he would be released because no one could ever prove that he had hurt his wife.

Through the years, Shue always maintained that he was an innocent man. He died in 1905 in the Moundsville Penitentiary.

Today many people would scoff at such a tale, but Zona's mother was not superstitious or uneducated. She was considered a pillar of her community, a good Christian woman, and someone not given to flights of fancy. Perhaps that was why she was so readily believed. The prosecuting attorney also was neither uneducated nor superstitious, yet he was swayed to believe that the spirit of the dead young woman sought justice. And then there were the twelve jurors who also believed that Mrs. Heaster was telling the truth. Erasmus Shue was convicted of the murder of his wife on purely circumstantial evidence.

In Greenbrier County today, a historical marker commemorates the death of Zona Shue. The story of her return from the dead and the conviction of her husband for her murder are part of the history of Greenbrier County. Zona's case remains unique in the annals of criminal law, because she was allowed to testify against her own murderer.

Kate's Last Stand

Did you ever wonder how it's possible for a story to survive even when the names of the people involved have long been forgotten? Perhaps it's because the story is so inspiring or passionate that most people can relate to it, and the feeling is so strong that the story endures. In the White Sulphur Springs area, just such a story is still passed on, although many of the names have been lost in the mists of time.

A woman known only as Kate, her husband, and their small son had come to Greenbrier County to build a new life around 1783. She and her husband were young and full of energy, and they wanted a good environment in which to raise their son. They had very little when they first arrived in the mountains of what was then Virginia, but they believed that they could carve a farm out of the wilderness and leave their son a legacy he would be proud of.

Kate and her husband worked hard. They cut trees to construct a little cabin and cleared enough land for a garden. From sunup until after darkness fell, Kate planted, hoed, weeded, cleaned house, did laundry, cooked, spun wool, and made clothing. She sat by the fire darning patches onto her son's breeches or knitting the wool into a warm shirt for her husband. But through it all, she had one overwhelming worry. She feared the Mingo and Shawnee Indians who lived in the area. The terrible resentment and anger that flared up between the settlers and the Indians often erupted in violence. Kate and her small family attempted to stay away from the conflicts. She and her husband wanted only to live peacefully and raise their son.

The fighting came in cycles. There were few attacks in the winter, but spring and fall were the worst times of the year in the mountains. The Indians would attack, kill, and burn one area, and the whites would do the same in another. The justification was always that it was in retribution for a previous attack elsewhere, but rarely did the people who actually committed the deeds get attacked in return. Usually innocent people were drawn into the fray. Any Indian would do when a settler was killed, and any settler's cabin would be fine when the Indians wanted retribution. It was a vicious cycle that drew many innocent people into its web of death and destruction.

One late summer night, Kate's worst fears came true. She awoke to the hair-raising sound of war cries and the smashing of pottery in her little kitchen. Her husband reached for his gun and shouted to Kate to gather up their small son. Kate knew that her husband was sacrificing himself so that she and their child might live. But she had no time to worry about that now.

Barefoot and in her old nightgown, she slipped through the back window and out into the night with her child. The little boy began to cry in fright, and Kate hushed him as she dashed madly for the woods. At the edge of the garden patch, something struck her in the back. Desperately, Kate whirled around and clawed for her child as he was roughly yanked from her arms. Hard hands grasped Kate's arms and pulled her hands away from her screaming little boy. Kate struggled to get to her son, but in vain.

Within moments, both Kate and her little boy were dead. Their bodies were horribly mutilated, their scalps were taken, and their heads were cut off and left nearby. Inside the house, her husband's corpse met a similar fate. Outside, hostile eyes watched the burning of the little cabin. Kate and her husband had taken a calculated risk so that they might better their lives, but like so many others, they lost the gamble and paid the ultimate price.

Shortly after the grisly murders were discovered, people began to refer to the mountain as Kate's Mountain. The position of the bodies told the local settlers all they needed to know. They understood the grim decisions that had been made that night and were aware of the desperate race Kate had run and lost as she tried to save her life and that of her little son.

Through the years, stories came down from many of the settlers who built their homes on the mountain. People talked about seeing a headless woman running frantically toward a grove of trees. Other people walking by the ruined cabin claimed to have heard the cries of a little child and the screams of a woman that were cut off prematurely. The area still carries Kate's name in memory of that long-ago tragedy, and perhaps the mountain will always be haunted by the spirits of Kate and her little boy.

Locals claim that the mountain holds other secrets as well. There have been reports of lights hovering above the trees and darting to and fro. Many people claim to have heard a humming sound coming from deep within the mountain. Even more bizarre, when the humming suddenly breaks the stillness of the air, car lights, windshield wipers, and radios suddenly come to life. No one knows why these electrical disturbances happen, though there are many theories about the humming deep within Kate's Mountain.

John Henry, the Steel-Driving Man

John Henry is an icon for the post–Civil War black man, and his story has been told in numerous versions of the song "John Henry." Many people doubt that he ever really existed, and he is most often associated with other mythical heroes such as Paul Bunyan and Pecos Bill. But unlike those characters, whose exploits were patently fictional, John Henry's story has the ring of truth.

After the Civil War, a vast pool of cheap labor came into the marketplace. All of the newly freed slaves had to find jobs, and they were willing to do dangerous work for little pay. Many industries exploited the desperation of these people, but no industry profited from the former slave labor more than the railroading industry. Building a railroad was dangerous work, and the railroads were looking for ways to lay track cheaply. They hired immigrant labor in the West and East, and in the South they took advantage of the freed blacks.

In Talcott, West Virginia, John Henry, a massively strong young black man, took a job on a work crew laying track through the mountains. John Henry's job was to drive steel bits into the solid rock while a man called a turner turned and replaced drill bits. The holes drilled into the rock would be filled with dynamite so that mountainsides could be blasted open and railroad tunnels driven through them.

The men who drove steel were proud of their hard work and took pride in how much steel they could drive. In fact, they often held contests to see who could drive steel fastest, and John Henry was the undisputed champion.

The C&O Railroad faced many obstacles while laying track across West Virginia, as the entire state is filled with mountains and valleys. Going over the mountains was sometimes cheaper and more viable, but at times it was determined that going through a mountain would be more cost-effective. That was what happened near Talcott, where the railroad decided to build a tunnel through the mountainside. It was an expensive and deadly enterprise for the railroad and its workers, and nearly a thousand men were killed in the making of the Big Bend Tunnel.

Rock slides, collapsed shafts, and other hazards claimed many of those who died. At one end of Big Bend Tunnel was a slag pile that had an evil reputation among the black workers. It was said that after some of the accidents in the tunnels, the blacks who were killed were tossed into the slag pile. Unfortunately, the stories of dumping dead black men in the slag pile were true. If ever a place should be haunted, the Big Bend Tunnel would be the place. But it is not the souls of those disrespected men who are said to haunt the tunnel. It is the spirit of John Henry who has been seen and heard there, and the tale of how he came to haunt the tunnel is what made him a legend.

As the story goes, a salesman came along and tried to sell a steam-powered jackhammer to the local railroad foremen. It was a forerunner of the pneumatic drill, and the salesman said that it was faster than any man could be. It didn't need to be paid and didn't need to take breaks. It didn't get sick and never slowed down. Machines were the wave of the future, the salesman said, and the foremen were impressed. The men laying track and building the railroad lines were very upset, however. Mechanization would put many of them out of work, and they were frightened of what it meant.

The men persuaded the bosses to have a contest. If a man could beat the machine, then the bosses wouldn't buy it. The bosses agreed to the contest. The men chose the best steel driver ever, John Henry, for the contest.

According to the song:

John Henry was hammering' on de mountain,
An' his hammer was strikin' fire,
He drove so hard till he broke is pore heart,
An' he lied down his hammer an' he died,

John Henry beat the steam drill, but his efforts caused him to die. Many people said that he died of a stroke, but the song says, "He broke a rib in his lef'-han' side, An' his entrels fell on de groun'."

In *Steel Drivin' Man: John Henry, the Untold Story of an American Legend,* author Scott Nelson makes a convincing case for the idea that John Henry was actually a real man. Nelson notes that during the slave years and just after the slaves were freed, the blacks would code messages into songs. A prime example of this was in the song "Follow the Drinking Gourd," sung throughout the South. The lines of that song were actually a coded message about how to get north to freedom. The story of John Henry, Nelson asserts, is quite probably true.

But Nelson doesn't stop with suppositions. He looked at the oldest versions of the song of John Henry line for line and soon saw patterns arising. The patterns all seemed to come together for him when he read in a newspaper about an old prison being torn down. He followed the story of the prison and learned that on November 16, 1870, a nineteen-year-old black man named John William Henry was sentenced to ten years in prison for "housebreaking and larceny." John Henry was sent to the Virginia Penitentiary, where he was contracted out as convict labor to work for the C&O Railroad. For 25 cents a day that was paid to the prison, John Henry and the other convicts did the hardest and most dangerous work. They were forced to breathe in deadly silica inside the mountains and go into dangerous areas to work. The infamous slag pile was the final stop for more than one of the contracted convict laborers.

If Nelson is right, then it was at Lewis Tunnel, near Big Bend Tunnel, that the race took place. According to the existing records, that was where steam drills were used along with manpower, because the rock was hardest there.

Following the song, Nelson found that in all probability John Henry was buried in an unmarked grave near the prison. During the razing of the old Virginia Penitentiary, three hundred bodies were dug up from an illegal cemetery near an old, white building on the penitentiary grounds that the convicts had called the White House. The building was used for several purposes, including as a morgue. The song records John Henry's death like this:

They took John Henry to the White House
And buried him 'neath the sand
And every locomotive come a'rolling by
Says there lies a steel driving man.

After the death of John Henry, the other workers soon refused to work in the tunnels. They claimed to hear his hammers clinking down on steel. Others said that they saw John Henry walking past carrying his two twelve-pound hammers as he went back to work. Even today people still report sightings of John Henry and claim to hear the sound of hammers slamming down on steel.

The Musician of Bud Mountain

Wyoming County, in southeastern West Virginia, is home to many folk stories and legends. Bud Mountain has long been associated with the legend of Berg Hammond. According to local folklore, Berg was a peddler who traveled through the area in a wagon pulled by an old team of horses. Berg lived in the wagon, sold his wares from the wagon, and apparently died in the wagon.

For homesteaders in the early 1800s, a peddler and his wagon were a great treat. The peddler brought news from other farms and often from distant locations as well. The wagon was filled with goods that the farmer could trade or purchase to make his life easier. The peddler was welcomed at each lonesome farm and homestead, where housewives craving news of the outside world would ply him with baked goods and hot coffee. He was often offered a meal and a soft bed or sweet haymow to sleep in. The housewife and her husband would look through the many goods that filled the wagon: bolts of cloth, bits of lace, new buttons, needles and thread, and other items that might make the housewife's life easier. And for the husband, tobacco, bags of seed to plant, and tools that might be used on the homestead.

Berg Hammond carried all of those items in his covered wagon, but he also carried a more precious cargo, in his estimation. Berg carried with him musical instruments for sale. At heart, Berg was a vagabond musician traveling like a gypsy across the rutted dirt roads of the mountains that are now West Virginia. He could play every instrument for sale on his wagon and often entertained farm families with an impromptu concert. Visits from Berg were pure joy for the folks along his route, and he was always treated well.

Berg was a fixture on those mountain roads for many years, and folks had grown to take him for granted, but one foggy, rainy night all of that changed. Berg had not found a good place to rest his weary old bones that night, and he was pushing on over the mountain in hopes that on the other side a kind farmer and his wife would take him in. It had been raining all that late fall day, and now the mountain road was awash in gray, misty fog. Berg and his horses plodded along as the wagon clattered over the potholes and ruts of the old dirt road. He promised himself that if no warm barn appeared soon, he would pull off the road at a wide spot on the far side of the mountain and rest for the night. He was having a difficult time seeing the road in front of him, and there were no lights to ease his way.

Suddenly the unthinkable happened, and Berg found himself off the narrow, winding track. The horses neighed in terror as they struggled to pull the heavy-laden wagon back from the muddy brink. Berg pulled back on the reins and tried to stop the wagon as he jammed his foot down on the brake. But the wagon slid despite his best efforts. Within seconds, Berg and the horses were lying dead at the bottom of the mountain along with the broken wagon.

It was days before anyone found Berg and the horses at the foot of a steep drop along the side of the mountain. Folks for miles around were devastated by the loss of the peddler and music man.

Soon folks began to say that on stormy nights, old Berg would go back to the mountain where he died to play his instruments once more. His favorite instrument was the fiddle, and many a sodden traveler over the years has claimed to hear its wild, mournful strands. Throughout his life, Berg would play whenever anyone asked him to, and some folks along Bud Mountain claim that if you ask Berg to play for you, he will saw on his fiddle once more.

A Wicked Wind This Way Comes

In rural McDowell County, the people are good, hardworking folks who don't dwell on the supernatural. Like many other people in rural Appalachian areas, they spend their time working, raising their families, and simply trying to survive.

In the 1940s, the area was even more rustic, and only a few locals had cars. Those who did were considered lucky and were expected to use them if necessary to help their neighbors in case of an emergency. Most folks didn't mind helping out; they considered it their duty to help someone if they could. A car could certainly get someone to the hospital faster than a horse and buggy would.

One local family was the Montgomerys, a young couple with three small children. Ray worked in the local mines, and Elva stayed home with the children. Staying at home did not mean she had nothing to do, for she raised a large garden, canned, and took care of the chores. There was a lot of work on their remote little farm, but with the long hours that Ray put in at the mines, he did not have much time to help out. On weekends, however, Ray tried to catch up on the heavy work that Elva could not do alone during the week.

Elva and Ray were going about their chores late one November afternoon when a neighbor girl came running up. The girl quickly explained that her mother was ill. She knew that Ray had a car and begged him to take her mother to the hospital. Ray didn't have to be asked twice.

The young couple tried to calm down the girl, reassuring her that in a few short moments Ray would be on his way to pick up her mother. Ray ran into the house and got his coat. He grabbed up the car keys and ran back out the door, calling to the girl to jump into the car. Elva ran after him, and he took her hand quickly. "Take care of the place, Hon," he said. "I'll be back as soon as I can." Elva gathered the children close to her and told Ray that everything would be fine, and then Ray was gone.

Elva turned back to her work while her mind worried about what was happening at the neighbor's house. From the sound of things, Ray would not be back for a long time. He would not abandon the neighbor children until he was sure that their mother or another relative could care for them. One of the things that Elva loved about Ray was his sense of duty. She knew that no matter what happened on the farm, she and the children would be just fine.

As the afternoon waned, Elva picked up a bucket and headed for the pump to bring in water for the night. The children tumbled out of the house around her to look for the prettiest fall leaves, while their mother pumped water into the big bucket and carried it inside for the night.

Suddenly a voice filled the air above her head. Elva looked up sharply, and the children fell silent as they listened too. It was a man's voice, and he was breathing heavily as if he had run a long distance. The voice was deep and had an urgency that frightened Elva. Quickly it began to tell her what she needed to do. Something about the voice made her want to listen to it. Perhaps she had an instinct that told her this voice was trying to protect her and her children. It told her to hurry to the house and nail the doors and windows shut. A great danger was rapidly approaching, and she had to protect the children and hide.

Elva gathered her children quickly and ran back to the house. In her panic, she could not find the hammer, and she cried out because she did not know what to do. Suddenly the voice was with her again and told her that the hammer and nails were in a box behind the front door. She ran to the door and flung it shut. There sat her husband's toolbox, with the hammer and a can of nails right on top. She grabbed it and frantically began to nail shut the windows. She did not even stop to think that what she was doing made no sense. She did not stop to consider where the disembodied voice came from, because somehow deep in her heart she knew that this voice spoke the truth and was trying to protect her.

Elva worked as fast as she could. She nailed every window shut within minutes as a frantic fear gripped her. Her children watched in wide-eyed wonder as their mother seemed to go crazy. She pushed a heavy dresser against the back door after it was nailed shut and hurried to nail shut the front door as well. She had the house as secure as she could make it. Not for one moment did she even consider that this was total foolishness. The entire process took less than fifteen minutes, but for her it felt as if it had taken hours. She felt the need to hide with her children before the terrible thing came. She did not know what the terrible thing was, but she knew that the voice was trying to protect her from it.

Elva glanced around the house, frantically looking for a place to hide. Suddenly her eyes fastened upon the heavy kitchen refrigerator, which sat in a tiny alcove, and she ran to it. With strength she did not know she possessed, she shoved the refrigerator forward. She called for her children, and they came running, because they too felt the sense of urgency that was driving their mother. She huddled down behind the refrigerator with the children in her arms and waited. She had no idea what she was waiting for, but she knew with certain conviction that this terrible something was just about to come.

Moments later, there was a sudden change in the air—a strange pressure like just before a storm. In the distance, she could hear what sounded like a mighty wind wailing, moaning, and moving closer to her. She hugged her children tighter and waited. Suddenly the wind hit the house, pulling at the rafters and tugging at the eaves. The wind seemed to rattle every window in succession as if trying to enter through them. Elva held the children tight and followed the progress of the wind mentally. She heard the back door shudder and prayed that it would hold. She had never experienced anything like this before. This wind brought with it the normal fear for safety that anyone would have, but it also brought with it a sense of evil. Elva could not have explained how she knew, but she knew that if this wind could reach her and her children, it would destroy them all. She also knew instinctively that this wind knew that she and the children were inside, and it wanted to hurt them. Perhaps it was more accurate to say that whatever the wind carried with it wanted to kill them.

Elva was paralyzed with fear, and the children seemed to sense it. They stayed perfectly quiet, their little bodies pressed against her as they waited for whatever was outside to make its way indoors. Elva heard the wood strain at the front door as the evil wind tried to gained entrance. Thankfully the nails and lock held, and the door remained blessedly closed.

Suddenly the wind whirled away as fast as it had come. Elva sensed that the danger was past, but still she could not move. Never before in her life had she been truly paralyzed with fear, but now she was. For a while, she could not think of what she should do, so she simply sat and prayed that the wind would not return. The children huddled with her; none of them made a sound save for the youngest daughter, who wept quietly against her mother's chest.

The darkness pressed in around Elva, but still she could not move. Finally she heard what sounded like a car in the driveway. She listened in apprehension as the motor died and the car door slammed. She followed the sound of footsteps as they rapidly approached the front door. Suddenly the door gave a mighty thud as if someone were trying to get in. The doorknob rattled, and she heard Ray's voice calling to her. Elva ran for the door and turned on the light. Then she grabbed the hammer and began to pry loose the nails.

When the door finally came open, Ray stared at the bizarre scene inside the house: the nail-ridden door, the windows nailed shut, and objects pushed up in front of the refrigerator, which was now far from the wall. Behind the refrigerator, he found his three frightened children. Elva began to cry and told him about the voice from nowhere, and the terrible wind and the evil feeling that it had brought with it. She told him how she had nailed the windows and door shut, and how she hid and waited for whatever was coming. She told him about how it had tried the doors and windows as if looking for entrance. Ray did not know what to say. His wife was a no-nonsense lady who was not prone to flights of fancy, yet she was telling him the most incredible story.

In the morning, Ray found evidence of his wife's veracity outside. Trees were mangled and twisted in a path around the house, and shingles lay strewn throughout the yard as if a tornado had touched down. All Ray could do was clean up the mess and thank God that somehow he had sent someone before the horrible storm to warn his family and keep them safe.

It is said that those who are kind and helpful have a special place in Heaven, but it may also be said that perhaps in this instance Heaven intervened to protect a family because they had helped another.

What happened on that horrible evening was so terrifying that forty-five years later, the family still speaks about it. Elva still wonders what fate almost befell her and her children, and the children remember the evening their mother hid them behind the refrigerator. As for Ray, all he knows is that thanks to the intervention of a disembodied voice, his small family was saved from some horrible fate, and for him that is enough.

The Horrible Specters
of Piney Bottom

Piney Bottom in Lincoln County is a remote and lonesome area, and it's easy to see why this place is the source of ghost stories. One apparition that stalks Piney Bottom is a headless man in black. This specter has been reportedly seen throughout Piney Bottom, but he seems especially fond of walking near the first little creek that winds through the area. Who the man is or how he came to be headless is a mystery.

But seeing the headless specter is not nearly as frightening as what some other folks experienced in Piney Bottom. Throughout the 1800s, there were scattered reports of a horrible beast encountered there. People riding their horses through Piney Bottom began to report that as they made the first crossing of the stream that ran across the bottomland, something heavy suddenly mounted their horses behind them. When they turned to see what had climbed aboard, they would find a headless black beast that appeared to be part human and part animal. Terrified, they tried to push the creature off but could not budge it. The creature rode along with them until they forded the next creek. It was a horrifying ride for the poor person, because the beast's arms were wrapped tightly around the rider, and the horse struggled in fear the entire time. As horses gave way to cars, accounts of this headless black creature faded away, but the stories are still told of something horrible that once traveled across Piney Bottom by hitching a ride on the back of some hapless person's horse. Some people speculate that the headless man in black and the headless beast are one and the same, but there is no way we'll ever know.

Mamie Thurman's Restless Spirit

Perhaps one of the saddest spirits in West Virginia is that of a young woman named Mamie Thurman. In 1932, most Americans had been devastated by the Great Depression. Jobs were scarce, money was difficult to come by, and people were just trying to survive. But in the small community of Logan, all of this was forgotten for a little while, because the small town was rocked by murder, scandal, adultery, and political intrigue.

Mamie was the wife of local patrolman Jack Thurman. She was a thirty-one-year-old dark-haired beauty with a sense of style. She was active in her church, had a lot of friends, and seemed to know many prominent businesspeople. Everyone was stunned when a young deaf-mute named Garland Davis found Mamie's body on a local mountain. Davis was picking berries on June 22 when he came upon her body on the side of Trace Mountain. She was a gruesome sight. Clad in a dark blue polka-dot dress, she still wore one shoe, and the other lay nearby. Her throat was slit from ear to ear, her neck was broken, she had a severe crack in her skull, and she had been shot twice at close range with a .38-caliber gun on the left side of her head. Someone had obviously wanted Mamie Thurman dead.

Robbery was immediately ruled out as a motive. When Mamie was found, she was still wearing her gold wedding ring, a white gold diamond ring, and an expensive watch. Her purse was a few feet away, and there was $10 in the wallet—a large sum of money for that time period.

The police arrested a prominent local banker and political figure named Harry Robinson and his African American handyman Clarence Stephenson. Soon the whole town was in an uproar, and rumors circulated that Robinson and Mamie had been having an affair and that Stephenson had been complicit in helping his boss pull it off. Some people speculated that Robinson had murdered Mamie in a lover's tiff. The townspeople were divided. Some folks tried to protect Mamie and her husband from the rumors, believing she was a churchgoing, God-fearing saint of a lady who was being maligned, but others labeled her a fallen woman.

The police never really considered Mamie's husband a suspect. Some folks claimed that it was because he was also a police officer, but soon even the most suspicious among them were silenced. On the day of Mamie's funeral, the state police executed a search of the Robinson home. In the basement, they found a small bundle of bloody rags and several bloody spots on the floor that had been quickly wiped up. Attempts had been made to hide what appeared to have been a bloody mess. They also found a razor and a small hole in the wall that looked like a bullet hole. Later a chemist determined that the blood found on the rags and in the basement was human blood, but blood analysis was not yet allowed in courtroom testimony, so the jury never heard it.

The police questioned a boarder who was staying with the Robinsons named Oscar Townsend. Townsend had worked at the bank with Robinson and had become friends with him and his wife. Townsend told the police that he had traded his .38-caliber handgun for the .32-caliber gun that Robinson had owned. Now they knew that a gun of the same caliber as the one that shot Mamie had been in Robinson's possession.

The state police inspected Robinson's car and found blood spots there as well as a clot of blood under a floor mat. An attempt had been made to clean up the car, but the blood clot had been overlooked because it was underneath the mat. The backseat of the car was missing, and a large tarp covered the back of the front seat and the area where the backseat should have been. A piece of bloody carpeting was also found.

Harry Robinson finally testified during his indictment hearing that he had been carrying on an affair with Mamie Thurman for more than two years. He stated that they often conducted the affair at an area club called the Key Club, where many prominent men and their secret lady friends met. Robinson went on to further besmirch Mamie's reputation, saying that he had been given a list of sixteen names of men with whom she had recurring affairs. He said that he had continued to have an affair with Mamie despite the fact that she had refused to give up the other men.

Throughout the hearing, Mrs. Robinson steadfastly maintained that neither Harry nor their handyman could have committed the crime. She seemed unfazed when confronted with the affair and informed the district attorney that she had known about it for some time. She stated that she and Harry had grown apart over the years but had remained friends. She hated Mamie because of the affair but had learned to accept it.

Mamie's husband maintained that to the best of his knowledge, his wife had been a good woman. He seemed brokenhearted by the whole thing, and one newspaper later called his testimony pitiful.

For his part, Clarence Stephenson steadfastly refused to offer any evidence that would incriminate his employer. In fact, he later pleaded with his sister to pass word to Mrs. Robinson that he had said or done nothing that would cause her or Mr. Robinson any distress. He seemed unconcerned, either believing that he would be vindicated or else already aware that he would be convicted for the crime.

Perhaps predictably, Harry Robinson was not indicted, but Clarence Stephenson was. The district attorney came up with a con-voluted theory that Stephenson was also having an affair with Mrs. Thurman. The idea of a black man having an affair with a white woman was enough to virtually guarantee a conviction.

After being convicted of the crime, Stephenson was sent to Moundsville Penitentiary. He later was transferred to Huttonsville Prison Farm, where he died of stomach cancer in May 1942.

The case of the murder of Mamie Thurman seemed strange, tragic, and mysterious in many ways. A lot of people believed that the wrong man did time for her murder, and that she never received justice. Perhaps that is true. Stephenson was rumored to have received his meals from a local diner instead of eating prison food. Warden Oral Skeens was said to have chosen Stephenson as his chauffeur. Later, a man who served time in prison with Stephenson claimed that the handyman told him he had been hired to take Mamie's body to the mountain where it was found. He swore that he had not harmed Mamie in any way. Stephenson also confided that the whole thing was "just politics."

Many questions were left about Mamie's life, lovers, and death. And even in death, she was not allowed to rest. Mortuary and cemetery records validate that she originally was interred at the Logan Memorial Park Cemetery in McConnell. The same funeral parlor also has record of payment to disinter Mamie years later and move her body to Crawfordsville, Kentucky, where her family came from. But there is no record of her ever being reburied anywhere in, around, or near Crawfordsville. Today no one knows what happened to her body.

In the 1980s, Mamie's half-brother, George Morrison, a retired district attorney from Albuquerque, New Mexico, contacted a local newspaper reporter named Dwight Williamson. Morrison had been a small child when Mamie was murdered, and he had known nothing of her or the crime until a few years before he contacted Williamson. The reporter became intrigued by the case and began researching it for a series of articles. He found that the court records of the trial and many other documents pertaining to the crime had disappeared over the years.

Today Trace Mountain is called 22 Mountain, and many people have forgotten about the brutal murder of Mamie Thurman. But some folks report having come in contact with her in a most intimate and frightening way. Mamie is said to walk along the road where her body was dumped. She is always seen in her dark blue polka-dot dress, with her curls carefully in place. She is a striking figure, and more than one person has stopped to offer this beautiful woman a ride away from the desolate spot where she stands. Mamie seems destined not to leave 22 Mountain, however. Although she seems to be seeking a ride, she always disappears from the car carrying her away from the mountain, returning to try again to escape the place where her body was so rudely dumped. Perhaps Mamie will have to eternally seek a ride back into Logan, since justice seems to have eluded her, and most of those who participated in her murder trial have already passed on to a more peaceful rest.

The Cornstalk Curse

The area that is today known as Point Pleasant was inhabited long before the first white man set foot on the land. Near the Kanawha River, it was always fertile ground. When white men first settled the land, they were faced with entire nations of people who had already established their homes along the river. Even then there were legends so old that no one could remember when they started. It was said that the Allegheny Mountains were haunted by ghosts and spirit people who could be dangerous to the natives if they were careless enough to anger them.

The Shawnee, Mingo, and Lenni-Lenape inhabited the area, and they were well aware of what the coming of the white man meant. They had lived through Pontiac's War years earlier and had been pawns in the French and Indian War. The local nations had sided with the British and tried to support the interests of their allies, who had warned the rebel Americans not to settle west of the Allegheny Mountains.

These three tribes had seen other native peoples driven out before the rising tide of land-hungry whites. Chief Cornstalk, a great leader among the Scioto Shawnee, came to believe that the best way to avoid being driven out by the whites was to make friends with them. He spoke of his hopes for friendship before the counsel fires, but many of the other chiefs disagreed with the chief. They believed that their only hope lay in showing the white men their strength. They wanted to fight for their right to live on their lands and for the interests of their British friends. Chief Cornstalk was frightened of the notion. He knew that a war between the whites and the natives would be devastating for his people. The whites had guns that killed with a blast. He had seen how bows and arrows fared against such weapons, and there was no doubt in his mind that the consequences for his people would be dire.

But in October 1774, many of the other chiefs gathered their forces together and attacked Fort Randolph, which was then commanded by Colonel Anthony Lewis. Chief Cornstalk felt that he had no choice but to support his own people in their bid to drive the whites out before they overtook the native lands, so with an army of twelve thousand men, Cornstalk attacked Fort Randolph. The whites had learned of the approach of the great army from some hunters who had sought refuge in the fort hours before the warriors arrived.

A terrible, bloody battle was waged. The men on each side were fighting for their very lives. Chief Cornstalk fought bravely alongside his men. Later the white survivors said that he had not only fought them with great courage, but also struck down several of his own men who had tried to run from the fight.

Chief Cornstalk had been right about the devastating effects of the guns against his men. Despite superior numbers, the chief and his warriors were driven back across the Ohio River by the day's end.

The chief was a great statesman, and he understood that the only survival he could hope for was that brokered through peace. To that end, he managed to broker a peace treaty with Lord Dunmore, who was in charge of the entire Point Pleasant area. Dunmore agreed to cease hostilities if Cornstalk and his nation would stay on the northwest banks of the Ohio River. Many of the local whites, including Colonel Lewis, felt that they had been betrayed by this deal, however. Nothing short of the death of every Indian on the Ohio River would satisfy them. They did not believe that they could trust a peace treaty with the natives. Cornstalk was considered a wily and intelligent leader, and they feared that he was setting them up for a devastating attack. Lewis spoke against Lord Dunmore's orders.

The American Revolution further complicated matters. The British pressed the Mingo, Shawnee, and Lenni-Lenape to attack the isolated farms, but Cornstalk realized that entering the conflict would only place his people clearly in the sights of his enemies, so he spoke against entering the battle. It was not a Shawnee fight, he warned his nation. The Shawnee should stay neutral. Despite the wise words of the great chief, many of the lesser chiefs felt loyalty to the British and decided to attack the Americans in the name of their allies.

On October 8, 1777, Chief Cornstalk and another chief named Red Hawk attempted to do an end run around the warring chiefs and rode into Fort Randolph under diplomatic terms. They spoke to the commander, Captain Arbuckle, and warned him that the majority of the Shawnee were going to side with the British. Cornstalk was also honest enough to say that though he did not wish to commit himself to battle, he would stand by the decision of his people and fight if he had to. He hoped that by warning the Americans, this could be avoided.

But instead of allowing Chief Cornstalk and Red Hawk to ride out under diplomatic truce as promised, Captain Arbuckle repaid Cornstalk's kindness and trust by having the two chiefs arrested. He told them that it was just an insurance policy against a Shawnee attack, as the warriors would not attack a fort where their own chiefs were held captive.

When the two chiefs did not return home, Cornstalk's son Ellinipscio came to the fort to check on his father. He learned the truth of the situation too late and was taken hostage too. For months the three men were kept against their will at the fort. Anger brewed within the Shawnee nation at the detainment of their chiefs. The warriors rumbled that an attack was the only way to free their leaders, but Chief Cornstalk counseled his people to remain calm. The prisoners were treated well, and he believed that patience would enable them to gain their freedom without bloodshed.

Unfortunately for the chief and his companions, one day a soldier named Gilmore was found scalped in the woods near the fort. It was obvious to all who saw the body that the man had been killed by Indians. His comrades were infuriated by the mutilation of their friend, and they set out to kill any Indian they saw. Talk quickly turned to Cornstalk and his comrades, who were in the stockade. A band of soldiers broke into the stockade despite being ordered to let the chiefs alone. Chief Cornstalk was riddled with bullets, and his son was also slain. Red Hawk was dragged out of the chimney flue where he had tried to hide and was brutally killed.

There are those who say that this act of brutality against wholly innocent men spawned a curse upon the land that is still working against Point Pleasant to this very day. As Chief Cornstalk lay dying, he allegedly cursed the land and the people. "I was the friend of the bordermen," he supposedly said. "Many a time I have saved him and his people from harm. I never warred with you save to protect our wigwams and our lands. I refused to join your pale-faced enemy. I came to your house as a friend, and you murdered me. You have murdered by my side, my son, the young Chief Ellinipsico." As those who watched the chief struggling in his death throes later described it, he seemed to calm and grow strong for an instant.

Then he turned toward his enemies. "For this may the curse of the Great Spirit rest upon this spot; favored as it is by nature, may it ever be blighted in its hopes, its growth dwarfed, its enterprises blasted, and the energies of its people paralyzed by the stain of our blood." With his last words, he gave up the ghost and fled his brutal companions for the society of the Great Spirit.

The men who murdered the innocents realized suddenly what a mistake they had made. They had committed murder. Some of them justified it by saying that they had only murdered Indians, but others knew that their crime had offended all that was good and natural.

Commander Arbuckle realized immediately that the situation was dire. He ordered the three men to be buried outside the fort walls. No one spoke of the evil deeds that were being covered up by the earth, but it did not take long before Cornstalk's nation learned of the great tragedy. They responded with a ferocity that was terrifying, beginning a war that lasted for seventeen years, until Mad Anthony Wayne ended it at the Battle of Fallen Timbers. During those years, the brutality and bloodshed on both sides were staggering. This was the first fulfillment of the Cornstalk Curse.

The idea that a bullet-ridden man would rise up to issue such a long speech does seem a bit far-fetched, but perhaps in some way Chief Cornstalk did curse the land, because Point Pleasant has a long history of tragedies and mysterious events. Fires, floods, and other natural disasters often befall this mountain town. In 1967, the Silver Bridge collapsed and took with it forty-seven lives. A mysterious creature called the Mothman is said to haunt the area, and sightings of UFOs are often reported in the air above Point Pleasant. Even an airplane has crashed at Point Pleasant, and a myriad of ghostly tales have been spawned by the tragedies visited upon this place.

Perhaps Chief Cornstalk did issue a curse, or perhaps he himself was the victim of an ancient curse that the Indians always believed lay upon this land. Long before the first white man came to West Virginia, the natives claimed that it was haunted land.

Even in death, Chief Cornstalk has had no peace among the whites. His bones were dug up twice. First they were buried at the County Courthouse, and later they were moved to the Tu Endi Wei Park alongside the Ohio River. Today a monument marks the remains of this great chief. The disrespect shown to Chief Cornstalk by having his remains moved about might itself have brought down a curse. Many native nations believe that disturbing the dead stops them from moving on, and they are forced to stay earthbound. The sheer volume of tragedies is enough to convince some people that Point Pleasant is stalked by a curse.

The Mothman

In the annals of West Virginia history, there is no story quite like that of the Mothman. The strange tale began in the fall of 1966, with a series of sightings of red glowing eyes near an old abandoned TNT factory and ammunition dump outside of Point Pleasant. The factory had employed people through both world wars to make explosives. But when the need for explosives diminished, the factory closed down. For years, the empty igloo-shaped buildings sat rotting away. The nine thousand–acre complex that had once been so busy was now reduced to a place where young couples hung out.

In the fall of 1966, however, things were about to change. People began to come back from the old TNT plant area with strange stories of seeing a large figure moving among the shadows, and they insisted that the figure had large, red glowing eyes. Within weeks, people would begin to find out what lurked within the environs of the old TNT factory.

On the night of November 12, 1966, newlyweds Roger and Linda Scarberry and another couple, Steve and Mary Mallette, were in the area of the TNT factory when they saw something rise up in front of them on the road. Red eyes glowed at them, and they saw a creature with wings folded against its back. Roger Scarberry was driving, and he hit the gas so that they could escape from the creature as fast as possible, but the creature stretched out its wings and flew upward above the car. The two couples heard a high-pitched squeal as the creature moved, and they noticed that it did not seem to flap its wings. As they sped down the highway, the creature stayed directly behind them. At times they were going seventy miles an hour on the twisting backroads, but the creature could not be shaken. It was not until they neared town that the creature broke off its chase. Two very frightened couples later reported their experience.

In the following months, many more people claimed to have encountered the Mothman creature, as a local reporter dubbed it.

In neighboring Wood County, only a few miles from Point Pleasant, people living in the Quincy Hill area of Parkersburg began to report hearing footsteps on the roofs of their homes at night. Rumor was rampant that the Mothman was traversing the rooftops of Parkersburg. People began to speculate that the strange creature was staying nearby, and many believed it was living in what they called "the Mothman's lair," a small cave at the bottom of Quincy Hill.

Throughout the winter, people reported finding strange, birdlike tracks in the snow near the munitions dump of the old TNT factory. Frighteningly, the tracks measured six feet apart. This would make the creature that made the tracks well over seven feet tall.

Those who saw the creature agreed on a general description. It was brown or grayish in color and six to seven feet tall, with a ten- to twelve-foot-long wingspan. The wings folded up behind the back of the creature, and it appeared to have no arms. The feet were most often described as clawlike and similar to those of a turkey or owl. The most terrifying feature of the creature was its incredible glowing red eyes. The eyes were huge, two to three inches across, and were not located in the head, but on the shoulders of the beast. In fact, the Mothman appeared to have no head at all, as none was visible when viewed from behind. The creature made long squealing noises similar to a giant mouse.

Over the next thirteen months, the creature was reported to have followed several different vehicles along the winding roads around Point Pleasant. Those who were chased by it were amazed at its speed. One man reported driving a hundred miles an hour and still being unable to shake the creature. Whatever this creature was, it seemed to not like bright light, for it always broke off the chase when the cars neared the lights of town.

During the period when the Mothman was most often sighted, the police and the local newspaper were also inundated with sightings of UFOs and what they called a big bird. In fact, the newspaper had to set up a UFO desk to handle all the alleged sightings. The fact that the UFO sightings happened at the same time as the Mothman sightings made people suspect that the two were related. Some people speculated that it was possibly a creature from another dimension. Yet another supposition was that the creature was actually the personification of Red Hawk, the Indian chieftain executed along with Chief Cornstalk in 1777, who had returned in retribution for his murder. The area was rife with theories. Everyone seemed to have a pet theory, and nothing seemed too far-fetched.

There was no denying that something bizarre was happening in the Point Pleasant area. The sightings continued throughout the winter, and many of them seemed credible. Other people who had seen the creature earlier finally decided to speak up as well. It was later estimated that from a hundred to two hundred people experienced sightings of the creature that year, but there is no way to validate the number. Some of the stories were quite compelling.

The first known sighting of the Mothman probably occurred on November 1, 1966, when several men from the National Guard armory at Camp Connerly Road reported seeing a large, brown figure in the trees. The guardsmen insisted that the creature looked humanlike but flew from tree to tree.

On the same day as the Scarberry sighting, five men who were digging a grave in a local cemetery saw a brown creature in the trees watching them. The creature had wings that it unfolded as it glided from tree to tree. The men were unnerved by the shadowy monster watching them at the edge of the cemetery and hurried to complete their task.

A woman named Connie Carpenter reported being chased by a humanlike creature that flew behind her car. She was terrified by her encounter and was sure that what she saw had not been a giant bird.

Tom Ury of Point Pleasant encountered the creature on November 10. He later insisted that the creature chased his car even though he drove at speeds upward of ninety miles an hour. This was the first known daytime sighting of the creature. Ury believed that what he encountered was a giant bird with a wingspan of approximately twelve feet.

The city of Point Pleasant was inundated with reports of the bizarre. UFOs were being sighted almost daily, and at night the Mothman was stalking the citizens. Credible witnesses saw giant birds flying through the sky. In nearby Gallipolis, Ohio, a crop circle was reportedly found. It seemed that there was no end to the oddities taking place late that fall.

On December 15, 1967, thirteen months after the first sighting of the Mothman, an event took place that would change Point Pleasant forever. About 5 PM that day, the bridge between Point Pleasant and Gallipolis, Ohio, known as the Silver Bridge, collapsed. Between rush hour traffic and Christmas shoppers hurrying home, the bridge was jammed with vehicles. Thirty-one cars were on the bridge when it collapsed, with sixty-seven people in those cars. Only eleven people survived the bridge collapse. Eight cars and two people who died in the collapse were never recovered. After that tragic event, sightings of the Mothman and UFOs dropped dramatically. People began to say that perhaps the Mothman had been a harbinger of doom, meant to warn them that tragedy was about to happen.

Officially, the local sheriff insisted that the Mothman phenomenon had been nothing but imagination and hype. He offered the theory that a migrating sandhill crane or snowy owl had been the cause of all the excitement. The sandhill crane had red feathers around its eyes and stood nearly six feet tall. But no one ever reported seeing a sandhill crane during the time of the Mothman sightings.

Looking back at the history of Point Pleasant, there have been other sightings of a birdlike humanoid creature. And each time such a creature was seen, a great tragedy was about to befall the area.

Today most people claim that the Mothman has gone back to wherever it came from, but some believe it is still out there waiting until a new tragedy is about to occur. Then it will reappear to warn of the tragedy and terrorize the people of Point Pleasant once again.

The Battle of Scary Creek

On July 17, 1861, the Confederate Army engaged Union troops in a battle along a little creek in Putnam County. Scary Creek, which runs through Teays Valley, would have been forgotten by everyone if not for that deadly battle—and for the fact that the area is now thought to be haunted.

When armies clash, they leave behind a great many problems that the local people must cope with. Buildings are damaged or destroyed, and fields of crops are ruined. But worst of all is dealing with the dead. In Gettysburg, Pennsylvania, twenty thousand dead men were left on the battlefields, along with dead horses and mules. At Scary Creek, the local people also were left with dead men who needed to be buried. It was the middle of July, so there was a need to rush as they dug graves in which to put the fallen.

It was only weeks after the battle when the first haunting was recorded. According to local lore, about three weeks after the dead were buried, people began to hear what sounded like a pitched battle going on at Scary Creek. Their first fear was that another battle was occurring in the same spot, but when they went to check, they found that nothing had been disturbed. The local folks were amazed that they found nothing amiss. The sound of gunfire and the screams of the dying had been so realistic that people began to whisper that maybe the area was now haunted. At night, strange lights were seen hovering above the battlefield and along the creek, men crying out for help and the sounds of battle were also reported. The men who had fallen at Scary Creek apparently were refighting the battle, and the area became known as haunted.

Over the years, the stories have died down, but occasionally someone wandering along the creek hears the sounds of a battle or sees a soldier in the distance, and the old tales are once more told. It seems that the dead did not rest peacefully after the Battle of Scary Creek and are still haunting the area to this day.

Mid-Ohio Valley

The Horrible Ghost of the Betts Farm

According to an article that originally appeared in the *Cincinnati Enquirer* two decades later, the home of Collins Betts in Grantsville in Calhoun County was the scene of a most disturbing haunting in 1864.

About three miles from the town of Grantsville lived a farmer by the name of Collins Betts. His home was a one-story structure located between the road and a stream that ran through his farm. Betts was well respected in the community and was considered above suspicion when a local peddler went missing near his farm. The peddler was known to have been carrying nearly $1,000 on his person when he left Grantsville. Several days went by before anyone realized that the peddler was missing. The last information known about the peddler was that he had been headed toward the Betts farm when he left town the morning of his disappearance. His body was later discovered in a shallow grave along the road not far from the farm. Betts was questioned, and he informed the sheriff that he had never seen the peddler that week. It was believed that on his way to the farm, the peddler was waylaid and killed for his money. Betts was never suspected of the crime.

Shortly after the body of the peddler was discovered, however, strange things began to happen in the Betts household. The family complained that they heard the sounds of water dripping into invisible tin pans throughout the house. The sound went on for hours, and grated on everyone's nerves. At other times, there was a terrible dull thud from one of the bedrooms on the second floor. Those who heard the sound said that it was as if someone had fallen in one of the bedrooms, but no one was ever found there. The entire family had the experience of having their bedding snatched off of them in the middle of the night, and objects often moved of their own volition.

One bedroom in the Betts home apparently became the focus of an evil entity. People sleeping in that room began to complain of paralysis and tightness in their chests. They would awaken with a feeling of suffocation and feel a heavy weight on the chest. Often they could not move their limbs, so they could not push the weight away, but on some occasions the victims did struggle and were able to move the object. Those who were able to see and touch the entity always described it as a large, black dog. As long as the huge dog remained on top of them, the people suffered the feeling of suffocation and the paralysis.

The Betts family appealed to the Reverend Wayne Kennedy, a friend who was a well-known Methodist minister who traveled throughout West Virginia. He volunteered to sleep in the haunted chamber in order to end the haunting. The following morning, Reverend Kennedy not only admitted defeat, but also had his own terrifying tale to tell.

According to Reverend Kennedy, at approximately 1 AM he awoke with a feeling that something was pushing down on his chest. He felt as though someone were trying to smother him. He attempted to calm down so that he might be able to address this problem and found that a large, black dog was sitting on his chest while he lay in bed. The *Cincinnati Enquirer* stated it this way: "He said that it was with the greatest difficulty that he was able to throw off the incubus and release himself from the deadly pressure."

When Reverend Kennedy left the Betts home the following morning, he stated emphatically that he would not spend another night in that haunted bedroom if he were offered the entire farm.

Although he was one of the first to experience this haunting, he was not the last to flee the farm.

Although the haunting centered on the one bedchamber, it was not confined to the house. A neighbor named James Wolverton and his adult son were driving their oxen team home from town one night when they had their own experience. As they climbed the hill near the Betts farm, they heard what sounded like a host of men riding hard toward them from the other side of the hill. Wolverton heard the metallic clank of swords inside scabbards and expected to see soldiers topping the hill. But at the top of the hill, he was horrified to see that the road ahead was clear although he and his son clearly heard troops riding directly at them. Just as the ghostly riders sounded as if they would run over Wolverton and his wagon, he cried out, "My God, men, don't run over me!" Amazingly, the sound of the phantom troops stopped at that very instant, and he and his son found themselves confused and frightened, but totally alone on the dark road.

One of Collins Betts's nephews experienced a different haunting on the same road that ran past the farm. He claimed that as he rode up the hill near his uncle's farm one night, a strange apparition frightened him and his horse so badly that he was thrown and the horse ran off, leaving him to fend for himself. The horse did not even return home the following morning and had to be found in the woods.

Even in the haunted bedroom, each member of the Betts family experienced the haunting in different ways. Some of them claimed to see horrible faces and phantoms coming at them. Others reported the oppression of the big, black dog. Perhaps the most dramatic and tragic experience the Betts family had was when Collins's brother John came for a visit and volunteered to sleep in the haunted bedchamber. Collins warned John about the haunting, but John declared that he was not frightened of haunts and would gladly sleep in the room. John was a big man, muscular, and able to take care of himself. He felt more than equal to the task of sleeping in a haunted room. He laughed and made fun of his brother and the family for their abject terror of the room.

That night, he laughingly went off to the bedroom and closed the door. When John did not come down to breakfast the following morning, Collins went upstairs to check on him. What he found was terrible. His once healthy brother was now paralyzed and barely able to speak. John told Collins that during the night, he had awakened to the feeling of suffocation and felt a heavy weight on his chest. He had been unable to move any of his limbs and had been forced to lie on the bed helpless throughout the night. Although he struggled to push off the weight, he was unable to control a single muscle, so he could not even cry out for help from his family nearby. The terrible oppression of his breathing and limbs had continued until the first light of morning. As the weight disappeared, he found himself able to breathe freely but still could not move a single limb. John left the Betts farm a broken man. He never quite recovered the use of his limbs, and he remained sickly after his night of terror.

Another neighbor stopped by to visit, and the Betts family offered to put him up for the night. This fellow had heard about the infamous haunted bedchamber, and he insisted that he be allowed to sleep there. Despite the many stories that the Betts family told him, he could not be dissuaded. He spent a most uncomfortable night, and in the morning he declared the room to be haunted and refused to ever stay in it again. But he was actually very fortunate, because his experience was not nearly as extreme as John Betts's had been. The neighbor claimed that throughout the night, he heard the sound of chairs being dragged across the bedroom floor, but when he would get up to investigate, there was not a single thing out of place.

Over the years, the house and its haunted bedchamber became infamous. People came from all around to see the house and hoping to stay in the haunted bedchamber. One of those who volunteered his services as a witness to the haunting was Captain Hayhurst. Afterward, he claimed that while he tried to sleep in the haunted room, a headless man arose at the foot of his bed. He was so terrified that he did not spend the entire night in the room, and in the morning he said he'd never stay in that house again.

Not everyone believed that the haunting of the farmhouse was due to the death of the peddler. Collins's sister once stated that the haunting had not started until old Mrs. Riddle, a neighbor of the Betts family, had died. There was no known animosity between the two families, however.

There is no record of what happened to the Betts family after they left their haunted farmhouse. The house became abandoned and eventually fell into ruin. Perhaps one of the most interesting facets of this unique haunting is that shortly after it began, the Calhoun County correspondent for the *Cincinnati Enquirer* chronicled the haunting in the newspaper. He interviewed dozens of people who claimed to have either experienced or witnessed the phenomenon. Interestingly, the stories of the horrible ghost of the Betts farm have not changed much in the intervening years. Perhaps no embellishment was needed with a haunting as frightening as this one.

The White Woman of the Silver Run Tunnel

In about 1870, a young engineer on the Silver Run route for the B&O Railroad became part of the folklore around ghost trains. The young man had been given the job of engineer aboard a westbound express. His train was to leave Grafton for Clarksburg and then continue on to Parkersburg. Near the town of Cairo was the Silver Run Tunnel. It was just like hundreds of other tunnels built by the railroad, but it would soon earn a sinister reputation.

On a clear evening with a bright half moon shining, the engineer was enjoying himself as he watched the train tracks ahead of him rush by. But just before the Silver Run Tunnel, he suddenly blinked in panic. Ahead of him, in the middle of the tracks, stood a young woman in a white evening gown.

The young engineer knew with sickening certainty that he would not be able to stop the train before it struck her. He had heard stories from older engineers of people who tried to commit suicide by jumping onto the tracks at the last minute and of bums who accidentally slipped and fell beneath the grinding wheels of the great trains. The young engineer reached out and grabbed the emergency brake and slammed the train to a halt. He quickly glanced ahead at the track, but it was bare other than the bank of fog that seemed to hang just before the entrance to the tunnel. The train's conductor hurried to him and demanded to know why the train had been halted. Shaken, the young engineer told his story, and the two men jumped off the train to look for what remained of the young woman.

Within minutes, the train was once again hurtling along the tracks, with the young engineer hoping that the young woman had stepped into the bank of fog and off the tracks in time.

The next evening, as the train neared the Silver Run Tunnel, the engineer began to scan the track for any signs of the young woman. Suddenly he saw her standing in the illumination from the central light at the front of the train. The young woman was wearing the same white evening gown, but this time the engineer was able to see more details. On her feet were what appeared to be gold slippers, at her throat was pinned a brooch, and her long black hair swung loose nearly to her waist. He could not help but think that she was very beautiful. At the same time, he was confused, because she was once again standing in the middle of the tracks. The engineer reached up and grabbed the emergency brake and pulled it for the second time. The train came screeching to a halt, and once again the brakeman and conductor hurried back to see why he had halted the train. The young engineer poured out his same story about seeing a young woman on the tracks between the train and a fog bank that seemed to hang at the mouth of the tunnel.

Once again the engineer and conductor got off the train to look, but there was nothing to see. The engineer was becoming frustrated, because he was losing time on this run, and he knew that the B&O Railroad valued speed for their trains. He climbed back aboard the train perplexed and a little frightened. Who was the young woman, he wondered. Why was she standing in the middle of the tracks? And how did she disappear without being hit by the train?

Over the next few weeks, the engineer began to quietly question other engineers who drove the Silver Run Tunnel route. None had ever seen the young woman, and this merely perplexed the young engineer even more.

A month went by, and he was beginning to feel that whatever he had witnessed on the tracks at the Silver Run Tunnel had been an anomaly. But one night when there was a half moon yet again, he found himself staring at the young woman once more. Erring on the side of caution, the engineer again grabbed the emergency brake and slammed the train to a halt. This time the conductor ordered a search of not only the railroad track, but also the tunnel, to see if someone was playing a prank on the young man. But nothing or no one was found.

By now the local officials of the B&O Railroad had heard about the ghostly goings-on and insisted that the young engineer be given a different job. They placed a man by the name of O'Flannery in his place. O'Flannery was a hard-bitten Irishman who had been an engineer for many years. Nothing seemed to shake this man, so the officials hoped they had put an end to the stories of the ghostly woman of the Silver Run Tunnel. O'Flannery heard the stories of the white woman and what had happened to his predecessor, and he vowed that he would not stop for her no matter what. At first he did not see the white woman, and he began to suspect that it had just been the young engineer's imagination. But one night after he been on the run for about a month, O'Flannery had reason to change his mind.

On that night, he was watching the tracks go by as the train began its ascent to the Silver Run Tunnel. He noticed a curious fog bank directly over the mouth of the tunnel, and as he stared at the fog, he suddenly realized that a young woman had just stepped out of it. The young lady was wearing a long, white evening gown, and she seemed not to notice that she was in the direct path of the train. O'Flannery pulled on the whistle and it blared loudly. To his surprise, he heard a loud moan near him. In that moment, O'Flannery reached up and grabbed the emergency brake and brought the train to a halt.

The engineer, brakeman, fireman, and conductor all began to search for the young woman, but they found nothing and no one. They returned to the train, but the conductor warned O'Flannery that his very job might be in the balance, and he should not pull the emergency brake again.

O'Flannery assured himself and others that if he ever saw the white woman again, he would run her over with the train before he pulled the brake and lost his job. For several nights, his resolve was not called into question, but one night he once again saw the strange fog bank and the young woman standing on the tracks. This time O'Flannery made a conscious decision not to stop the train or slow down. Instead, he allowed the train to pick up steam as it neared the tunnel and ran straight through her. Although O'Flannery had vowed he would run the woman over, the thought of perhaps having killed her rattled him considerably, and by the time he reached the railroad station in Parkersburg, he was a jumble of nerves.

As O'Flannery brought the train to a halt at the Parkersburg station, a large crowd of excited people gathered around the Silver Run Tunnel train. Some of the railroad workers informed O'Flannery that all along the route from Silver Run Tunnel, workers had reported seeing a young woman sitting on the cowcatcher on the front of the train. The great headlight from behind her had illuminated the young woman, and she had been clearly seen riding all the way to Parkersburg. Just as O'Flannery was pulling the train into the station, the front end of the train seemed engulfed in a small fog bank, and when the train came out the other side, the young woman was gone.

All of this was too much for O'Flannery, who had a nervous breakdown and refused to run the Silver Run Tunnel route again. The officials of the B&O Railroad never forced him to, but they did demand an inquiry into the matter, hoping for an explanation for the apparent haunting.

What they found out was less than comforting. Their investigators learned that twenty-five years earlier, a young woman on her way home to her fiancé had disappeared on the evening Silver Run Tunnel route. No one had ever heard from the young woman again. Her complete disappearance had baffled her family and friends, who knew that she had been looking forward to her wedding.

Years later, the skeletal remains of a young woman were found in a house at the edge of the little village of Silver Run. Did the remains of this young woman have anything to do with the haunting? Perhaps they did, because it is said that after the young woman's remains were removed from the building, the spirit of the woman in white was never again seen at the mouth of railroad tunnel.

In 1980, the Silver Run Tunnel was abandoned by the railroad system. Today it is part of a bike trail that runs through the area. No one reports seeing the young lady in white anymore. But there are bikers who will tell you that it is an eerie and lonesome area near this overrun tunnel, and they believe that long ago this area just might have been haunted by a woman in white.

The Spirit of Bessie Bartlett

Many of the homes in historic Parkersburg have interesting stories to tell, but one house on Ann Street holds a tragic secret. A prosperous dentist named Dr. Bartlett built the house in the 1870s. Dr. Bartlett's family lived in the house, and he had his dental practice there as well. He and his wife had several children, among them daughter Bessie. The family was quite fortunate until the summer of Bessie's tenth year, when a typhoid epidemic swept through Parkersburg and Bessie became one of the victims.

Dr. Bartlett and his wife were devastated by their daughter's illness. They knew that many of those stricken by typhoid fever would not recover. The doctor had other concerns as well. If it were known that his little daughter had typhus, then his patients would no longer come to see him. The city was in a panic, and anyone who had typhoid fever in their home would be quarantined. Worse yet, Dr. Bartlett knew that if anyone found out about Bessie's condition, they would insist that he take her to the local hospital. He did not want to leave his child alone with strangers to care for her. He believed that the best hope for Bessie's recovery was for him to attend to her himself.

The Bartlett family made up a room in the basement of the house where Bessie could stay. Typhoid fever caused a horrible spike in temperature, and the doctor hoped that the cool basement would break the child's fever. He carried Bessie to the basement and left her there. Dr. Bartlett and the family tended her to the best of their ability, but Bessie soon slipped away from them.

When the Bartlett family sold their home, the story of Bessie and her tragic death faded from memory. It was not until a century later that the story of Bessie and her father resurfaced in a most unlikely way.

In the 1980s, a family was driving through historic Parkersburg one day when they saw a For Sale sign in front of an old house. Something about the house seemed to call to the family, and they quickly decided to take a tour of the property. The father took along a camera so that he could take pictures of the interesting features inside the structure. He, his wife, and their little girls met the homeowners at the house and began the tour. The man snapped pictures throughout the house and even took some pictures in the basement. To his great surprise, when the film was developed, he saw what appeared to be a little girl in the basement. The child's image was faded out in places, but it was clear enough that they could see a little girl in a white dress in the basement.

This photograph more than intrigued the family, and they began to research the history of this house. They learned that Dr. Bartlett had built the property and also uncovered the story of Bessie, who had died in the basement of the house during a typhoid epidemic. They came to believe that what they had captured in the basement was the spirit of little Bessie Bartlett. Perhaps she had appeared to them because they had their own young daughters with them the day the photograph was taken.

There is no history of the Bartlett House being haunted until after the photograph was taken in 1980s, and skeptics would say that imagination took over at that point. But one is left to wonder at the strange photograph, as well as the curious stories of moving objects and the sounds of someone in the basement when it is unoccupied. Does Bessie Bartlett haunt her former home? Judging from the photograph that was taken, she seems to still be waiting for her parents to come and take her back upstairs with them.

The Haunted Blennerhassett Hotel

The Blennerhassett Hotel sits at the juncture of Fourth and Market Streets in downtown Parkersburg, and few people pass by the grand old hotel for the first time without stopping to admire it. A West Virginia oilman, Colonel William N. Chancellor, built the hotel in 1899 in grand Victorian style, with turrets and ornate gilt that awes the modern eye. In fact, Colonel Chancellor was responsible for building many fine homes and businesses in the Parkersburg area near the turn of the twentieth century. Today, however, his home, still owned by his descendants, and the fine old hotel known as the Blennerhassett Hotel are all that remain of his creations. But the hotel speaks well for Colonel Chancellor, and he seems pleased with it.

The hotel was considered the grandest hotel in West Virginia in its time, and people from all over the nation vied for the opportunity to stay in one of its fifty rooms. Through the years, the grand lady saw all that there was to see of human life. Romances, business deals, families traveling, and so much more occurred within the Blennerhassett Hotel.

Times and tastes change, and eventually the Blennerhassett Hotel fell out of vogue and the building was used for other purposes. First it became the First National Bank of Parkersburg, and then it was remodeled into a restaurant. But time and age took their toll, and eventually the building was abandoned. In the early 1980s, the old hotel was slated to be demolished. It was saved, however, and became a hotel again in 1986.

Today the hotel has once again earned a reputation as one of the finest hotels in the area. It has earned another reputation as well—as one of the most haunted places in Parkersburg.

Several entities seem to make this establishment home. Colonel Chancellor is seen and smelled in the building quite often. Dressed in a brown suit and with a thoughtful look on his face, Colonel Chancellor keeps track of the doings at the hotel. He is almost always seen when the hotel is undergoing renovations. He appears throughout the building, often seen on the second floor, both in the hallway and in the guests' rooms. People have told the desk clerks that they were awakened in the middle of the night to find a man watching them sleep. The man usually is standing near the foot or side of the bed, and he certainly has startled a few folks. He does not mean any harm, however. Perhaps he's just checking in to see how they like his hotel. He also puts in appearances in the front lobby of the hotel, where the front desk used to be, as well as the library and the dining rooms. He seems quite busy keeping watch over the running of the hotel.

Not only is Colonel Chancellor himself seen, but his cigar smoke is smelled and seen throughout the hotel. West Virginia prohibits smoking in public buildings, but the staff often report walking into the library to find it filled with the pungent aroma of cigar smoke, and they often see the smoke hanging in the air. Staff and guests alike have been treated to the smell many times, as it suddenly wafts through bedrooms, hallways, or around guests in the front hall.

How do they know that the man who smokes is Colonel Chancellor? On occasion the smoker has been sighted. He is always described as a tall, slim man sporting a full, bushy mustache and wearing a monocle. In case there is any doubt, people often pick the man out from the picture that hangs in the hotel.

The picture itself is interesting, because people have reported seeing gold lights dance around it, and the lights have been captured in photographs. One other oddity about the picture does seem fitting. People reportedly have taken photographs of the portrait and found a little glowing red light like the end of a cigar jutting from Colonel Chancellor's mouth. Apparently Colonel Chancellor was quite fond of his cigars.

Colonel Chancellor seems to favor the library, and he apparently enjoys not only reading the books, but tossing them too. On many occasions the staff have come in and found numerous volumes of the antique books pulled out on the shelves. They also hear crashes in the library and find that someone has thrown a book across the room. In fact, one particular book seems to be a popular object of derision. This maroon volume has been weighted down by a potted plant to keep it from careening into walls, but even that does not always stop the Colonel from hurling it across the room. Why he would be throwing the valuable old books is anyone's guess.

Colonel Chancellor is only one of many spirits at the Blennerhassett Hotel. Female voices are often heard whispering over the intercom system or microphones hooked up for special occasions. Another ghostly woman screams shrilly into the system, causing terrible reverberations in the equipment. Then she laughs loudly at her own antics.

A chef in the hotel reported seeing a little boy of around nine years old, dressed in what appeared to be 1920s attire, standing in the kitchen watching him one night. When the chef did a double take, the child was gone. Other staff members claim to have encountered the child in the basement near where the staff lounge area is located. The child is only glimpsed before he fades away.

The security staff has reported 1920s-style "flapper" music coming from the Charleston Room and ballroom music coming from other ballrooms. In the Charleston Room, staff members have also reported seeing the chandelier swinging, and silverware will not stay put on the tables of that room. They have a difficult time setting up early for parties, because on occasion the silverware will all be switched about so that someone is obliged to return the place settings to the right spots.

According to published reports, a phantom guest stopped by one night and frightened one paying customer. The customer said that he had gone to bed and had fallen asleep straightaway. He awoke when he felt the bed depress as though someone had sat down on the foot of it. The startled customer quickly looked at the foot of the bed and to his horror saw an old man sitting there. The old fellow looked directly at the customer and said, "I was here first," before he faded away. The customer was understandably no longer sleepy and didn't desire to stay in his room much longer.

The staff have long known about another spirit, whom they call the Four O'clock Knocker. Where the original front desk sat there is now a coffee shop. On occasion at precisely 4 AM, three loud raps have been heard on the wall near the doorway into the office. No one has any clue when he'll strike again.

A phantom maid has been seen scrubbing the front lobby where the check-in desk used to be. In her black-and-white costume, she hurries along doing her eternal work.

Perhaps the oddest spirit to haunt the hotel is that of the kissing bandit. Over the years, many women have complained of being awakened by little kisses raining on their faces and lips. As soon as they sit up, the kisses stop, and they find themselves alone and a bit confused.

The security staff has been treated to the sounds of a group of children singing above the piped-in music that plays in the hotel lobby. There is never a rational explanation for the sounds. One female staff member reported that she heard the phantom children sing "Jingle Bells" one night just before Christmas.

Even the elevators seem to have a life of their own. Guests often report that they push the buttons to get to their floor, but the elevator makes other stops along the way. No one gets on or off at the stops, so who is playing with the buttons? More mysterious is the fact that the elevator often goes from the second floor to the lobby and opens up for no reason. Is Colonel Chancellor getting a lift from his favorite haunt back to the lobby?

The hotel seems to have even imported a couple ghosts from elsewhere. The hotel purchased two large, stylish mirrors made from the salvaged remains of two mirrored door casings from a Victorian-era building torn down in New York City. One night a bar full of customers saw the reflection of a dapper man in a 1920s-style white tuxedo walking along. Folks turned to see the man in his unusual costume, but he was not there—although his reflection still was.

One afternoon the reflection of a sea captain was viewed in one of the other mirrors made from those doors. The man appeared almost in black and white, except for the brilliant shine of his brass buttons. Apparently the captain had been proud of those shiny buttons.

Ghost for ghost, the Blennerhassett Hotel holds its own. The ghosts there are quaint and funny, quirky and mischievous as they interact with the living, and they never allow the hotel to become a dull place.

Mountain Lakes

Twistabout Ridge

A legend as twisted as the ridge itself has long been associated with this area in Clay County. According to local lore, a man came to live on the ridge. He brought with him his pregnant wife and another young girl who cooked and cleaned for him. It soon became evident that the young servant girl was also pregnant, and local speculation immediately had it that the man was the father of the second unborn child. People spoke out against the man, calling him a bigamist and an adulterer.

When the wife grew ill and the other young woman was not able to attend to her any longer, he was forced to turn to the community for help. The local physician recommended a young woman who had done nursing work for him many times. The man up on Twistabout Ridge seemed to have money, and he hired the young nurse that the doctor recommended.

The community was up in arms that one of their young women was living with the adulterer and his two "wives." Although her friends and family were growing increasingly upset, the young nurse announced that she would have to move into the house on Twistabout Ridge so that she could care for her patient full-time.

Within a couple months, the young nurse was seen around town and out along the ridge more and more often with the man who had hired her. It was said that he was no longer allowing her to care for his sick wife. In fact, people in the town were beginning to suspect that the young nurse had joined the unholy liaisons that were going on in the house on Twistabout Ridge. Soon the suspicions of the townspeople were confirmed when the younger woman who had come to the ridge with the couple admitted that she was pregnant by her employer. Matters grew worse when the nurse told her family that the woman she had been hired to care for had died, but that she would not be returning to her home. She wanted to stay on the ridge with the servant girl and her employer.

Soon after the nurse announced that her charge was dead, the man and the nurse got married. The young woman who had traveled to Twistabout Ridge with the man gave birth to her child, but still she remained a silent part of this strange household. The nurse also gave birth to a baby a couple months later, but her child was stillborn. Throughout the next several years, she became pregnant repeatedly, but she never carried a child to term. Local people said that such a misfortune befell her because she had helped murder her husband's first wife.

Perhaps there was truth to the fact that the first wife was murdered, because soon after her husband remarried, stories began to circulate that a ghostly woman was seen along Twistabout Ridge who would vanish when approached too closely. The strangest thing about this woman was that she was pregnant and her tongue was horribly swollen, making her face deformed. People who saw her said she bore a striking resemblance to the dead first wife.

Up on the ridge is an old cemetery, now abandoned, where the nurse's stillborn and premature babies were buried. It is said that the cries of feeble infants are heard there, and others have reported seeing the woman with the swollen tongue.

Another spirit of a forlorn woman is also said to haunt the ridge. She was an elderly lady who in some way offended her neighbors. Her crimes were not recorded in history, but the fate that befell her was: her neighbors stoned her to death for her sins. After she was buried, her cabin was sold. Its new owners soon learned that although the woman was dead, she was certainly not gone. On many mornings, the family would awaken to find the front door not only wide open, but also propped open by piles of stones. Those residing in the cabin could not forget the woman's fate, for she was constantly leaving piles of stones about the place. Others reported that she dropped stones from the ceilings of the house, and that no one would stay there long for that reason.

Near the old cabin where the woman was stoned to death, there was a swampy place with a sinister reputation. At the edge of the swamp stood a large, old tree that was once known as the hanging tree. Legend has it that local criminals were hanged on that tree long ago. People still report seeing balls of white light hovering near the tree or up in its branches and hearing the sound of a body thudding to the ground.

Twistabout Ridge is a lonely place filled with shadows and legends, secrets and ghosts. It is a beautiful place to visit in the daytime, but at night the phantoms seem to come alive in the dancing shadows at the edge of the trees. Only the stalwart would want to venture into the woods here after dark.

The Ghostly Hitchhiker

In 1933, people counted themselves fortunate to have a job. Because of the Great Depression, unemployment was staggering and some people were starving to death. For Hank Collier, things were not that bad, however. He was young and had a job that he really enjoyed. He was a traveling salesman, and it was an adventurous life.

Hank was working in the Muddlety area of Nicholas County one week. Spring floodwaters had swollen the creeks, making it difficult for him to complete his rounds. Worse yet, it had been raining steadily for nearly a week. Most of the roads had turned into mud puddles, and crossing many bridges risked one's life. But Hank still enjoyed his work and made his way from one stop to the next.

Late one afternoon, Hank was making his way along a rutted dirt road when he saw a young woman ahead waving at him. She was bundled in a heavy coat, and he could barely make out her pretty features as the rain washed across his windshield. But Hank was a gentleman, and he could not pass by the young woman without offering to help her. Stopping the car in the middle of the road so that he would not get mired down, he rolled down his window and offered the young woman a ride. She promptly accepted it.

The girl slid in beside him on the passenger side and shuddered from the cold and damp. Her small face smiled up at him as she thanked him for the lift. Hank smiled back and thought how pretty she was. She had long, blond curls that lay flat and wet against her cheeks and large, brown eyes that reminded him of a young doe. Her smile seemed infectious on that rainy afternoon.

"I sure thank you, sir," she said, grinning up him. "I thought for sure I'd have to walk all the way home. I live just up the road a bit, but we'll have to take a detour because the bridge ahead is out."

For a man in Hank's line of work, detours were a hindrance. Delays cost him both time and gas, but what he minded most about detours was getting lost. The young woman beside him chatted amiably while he drove. He asked her if she knew how to get around the washed-out bridge, and she gladly volunteered to direct him. She told him her name was Ida Crawford, and she lived in a house not far away. She quickly routed him around the washed out bridge and down yet another old road that led them back to the highway. Once they were on a paved highway again, it did not take long for her to direct him to her home. It was growing dark by the time he pulled into her driveway, so Hank said a quick good-bye and hurried on his way. He paid little attention to the young woman as she got out and ran toward the house.

Down the road several miles, he pulled up at a grocery store that was on his route. The rain kept a steady rhythm as he hurried inside to speak to the shop owner. The store was redolent with the scent of burning wood, and several old men were gathered around a wood stove in one corner of the room, feeding it from a supply of wood near the backdoor.

One of the old fellows called out to Hank and asked him how the road was. Hank quickly told them about the washed-out bridge and how lucky he was to have picked up a young woman who knew a detour around it. Suddenly he had the attention of the whole group of old men, but Hank could not understand why his story interested them so much.

One old man sat up in his chair and looked at him carefully. He asked Hank to describe the girl, and Hank did so. The old men exchanged a glance and nodded. The spokesman smiled and asked if the girl had given her name.

Hank thought for a second and said, "Yes, I think she said her name was Ida Crawford. Do you know her?"

The spokesman nodded slowly. "Yes, son, we all know her. You best sit down, boy. I think you are gonna be a bit surprised by what we're gonna tell ya."

The old man eyed his friends sharply before he began his story, and someone pushed a chair in Hank's direction. Hank grabbed the back of the chair but did not sit down. He felt as though he were pinned to the floor.

The old man rubbed his chin as if choosing his words carefully. "Well, Ida Crawford grew up around here about twenty-five years ago. She was a pretty little thing just like you described her, with long blond hair, big brown eyes, and a smile that just made you want to smile right back. She used to drive around in a little buggy that her pap had made her. It was about this time of year when she had her accident. Just like this year, the spring melt and the spring rains came at the same time, and all the creeks and streams were flooded. Ida was on her way home from visiting a friend when she came to that bridge she told you was washed out, but she didn't know that the bridge was under so much stress. She drove her little buggy out on the middle of the bridge, and then the bridge collapsed. They found part of the carriage downstream, but no one ever did find Ida's body. A couple years went by, and then a young fella came through here and told a story just like yours. He said that he had been driving along the road during a flood, and Ida flagged him down. He offered her a ride and she showed him the detour that she showed you today. He took her home, too, only to find out later that she'd been dead for couple of years.

"There was one other fella after that whom Ida also helped. Anytime that bridge washes out, she seems to keep a sharp eye out for folks who might get hurt on it. Son, you are the third fellow that Ida has saved from that washed-out bridge."

Hank stared at the men for just a moment. He could barely believe what he had just heard. Ida Crawford had seemed to be a very real girl and not a ghost. He thanked the men and turned to leave.

Outside, he sat his car for about fifteen minutes trying to calm down. There was no way he had driven a ghost home, and he simply refused to believe such nonsense. Those old men were pulling his leg, and he was going to prove it. He pulled out of the grocery store parking lot and turned the car back the way he had come. He would go to Ida's house and see for himself that she was perfectly real.

Within moments, he was sitting in the driveway of the old house where he had dropped Ida off. Even though it had been raining heavily when she had left the car, he knew that this was the place. But now the headlights revealed an old, abandoned house. He got a flashlight from his glove compartment and turned it on. The house was dark, but he reasoned that a lot of folks lived without electricity because they could not afford it. Just because the house looked abandoned did not mean it really was. Perhaps the young woman lived there alone and was a squatter in the empty house without anyone's knowledge.

Hank entered the old house and flashed his light all around. He called out Ida's name, but no one answered him. There was no sign that anyone lived there. A few pieces of old furniture lay abandoned and forgotten on the floor, and the ragged remains of some ancient curtains flapped in the breeze. The only footprints that disturbed the dust were those of the wild creatures that now made the empty house their home.

Suddenly Hank no longer felt like looking for Ida. He hurried back to his car and sat there staring at the house for some time. Could it be possible that he had given a ghost a ride home? And had she saved him from driving off a washed-out bridge because of his kindness? If you talk to some of the old folks in Nicholas County, they'll tell you that Ida still remains there waiting for another spring flood—and another driver who needs to be saved.

A Cry for Help

In the late 1800s and early 1900s, tuberculosis was a terrible health problem. In some states, every county had a tuberculosis sanatorium to house the ill. Tuberculosis was called consumption or galloping consumption because it killed rapidly. The disease caused people to have difficulty breathing, have chronic coughing spells, and eventually cough blood from their lungs. It was often fatal.

In the early 1900s, physicians began to make progress in their war against this horrible disease. They learned that cold, damp weather offered the disease a breeding ground. Private sanatoriums sprang up in the Northeast and in Canada that offered a "cure" for the disease. Eventually tuberculosis was vanquished by the creation of a vaccine, but many people survived the illness because their families sent them to more appropriate climates.

A wealthy man from Connecticut was devastated to learn that his only child was stricken with consumption. He consulted a physician, who told him that his teenage daughter would have a better chance of survival if removed to a cool, dry climate. He contacted his brother, who lived on Point Mountain in Webster County, West Virginia, and asked him if he would care for the sick girl. Believing that his child would be in the good and loving hands of his brother, he promised to pay for her room and board.

When the young lady arrived in Webster County, she found that her uncle lived high in the mountains in a small house. She brought with her $1,500 that was to be used for her room and board as well as any medications or physicians that might be needed. She told her uncle that her father had promised to send $2,000 more in a few weeks to help pay for her medical care.

She found her uncle to be a taciturn man, but she attempted to win him over with kindness. The man was jealous of his brother's money and good fortune, so he determined that he would wait until his brother sent the remaining $2,000, and then dispose of his niece. He did not want his brother to find out that he had absconded with the money, so he decided he had to kill the young girl.

Once the money had arrived, he attacked the girl and killed her. He hid his crime by burying her body under the hearthstone of his fireplace. He then sold the property and left to go west.

The new owner was less than pleased when he moved into the house and found that it was haunted. The front door of the house would not stay shut, no matter what anyone did. He tried bolting it shut, wedging it shut, and even nailing it shut, but still the door opened and closed of its own volition. There also were sounds in the house as if someone were struggling, and heavy thuds and bumps.

It did not take long for the first family to move out. Eventually the property came into the possession of a local man who told his story about its being haunted to two friends who were elderly Christian ladies from his church. The two ladies surprised the man by telling him that they would stay in the house if he would provide them with a bed and a fire to keep them warm. They believed that whoever was haunting the house needed their help, and they would stay until they had contacted the ghost to find out what it needed.

Faced with the prospect of a house he could not use, the homeowner was more than happy to oblige the two old women. This was the first time he had even considered that there might be a way to contact and appease the ghost.

The homeowner set up a bed in the main room of the house and moved in a large stack of wood so that the ladies could stay warm. He made sure that the old wood stove was functional, and then contacted the two Christian ladies. On the appointed evening, the two women made their way to the house and locked themselves in. They were determined that they would stay awake until the ghost appeared so that they could ask the spirit what it needed.

They built a fire in the wood stove and settled into the big, old bed to wait. Late that night, they began to hear the sounds they had been told about. There were thumping and dragging sounds as if somebody had entered into a scuffle and had been knocked down. Then the door flew open, although it was locked, and the two old women sat up in bed.

No one before them had ever stayed after the door had flown open. But the old women were not frightened, believing they had the might of God on their side, so they sat and waited to see what would happen next.

To their surprise, a young girl no more than sixteen years old came into the room. She was frail and delicately built, and she seemed ill. Pity filled the two old women for the plight of this young ghost girl, and they asked her gently why she haunted the house and what she needed so that she could rest.

The girl poured out her story about her vengeful uncle. She told them about her illness and the doctor's diagnosis, her father's letter, and how she had come in good faith to get well. She told them about the money and how her uncle had murdered her. She told them that her body lay beneath the hearthstone where he had placed her so rudely only a few years earlier. She asked them for a

Christian burial, and then the young girl seemed to grow exhausted and faded away.

The two old women waited through the night, and in the morning they told the homeowner about the ghost child. The police were called, and they pried out the hearthstone of the old house, to find the remains of the young girl wearing the same color dress as the old women had described. The girl's father was contacted, and she was sent home to Connecticut for a proper burial.

The murderous uncle was located out west and brought back to West Virginia, where he was tried and convicted for the murder of his niece. The man was hanged for his crimes and the house was no longer haunted, because the two old women had answered the young girl's cry for help.

The Thunderbird of Owl Head Mountain

Thunderbirds are creatures of Native American mythology. They are great birds with a wingspan of eighteen to twenty feet, and the flapping of their wings was said to give off a thunderous sound. They were most often seen just prior to thunderstorms, so the natives believed that they brought thunder with them. If there was any truth to the stories of these huge birds, the air just before a thunderstorm is denser, so the heavy birds riding the air currents would be able to swoop farther down and ride the denser currents.

Stories of the thunderbirds, which were said to carry off humans, were told to the first white settlers, but they scoffed at the naive stories of the natives. Everyone knew that giant birds that carried away children were only nightmare myths—that is, until some frantic white men spotted the birds. Then suddenly the stories of the thunderbirds were seen in a whole new light.

On the mountain known as Owl Head in February 1895, an entire mountain community lived through what sounds like a horror movie, but for the poor people of Owl Head Mountain, it was all too real. When a child goes missing, everyone panics, and the families around Owl Head Mountain immediately came out to help look for little Landy Junkins of Bergoo. Ten-year-old Landy had been sent to ask after the health of a family friend, Mrs. Warnick, who lived a

couple miles distant. When Landy did not return from her errand, her parents grew worried. Her father went out to fetch the child. It had snowed the night before, and he could clearly follow his daughter's tracks along the familiar path toward the Warnick home. About a quarter mile before the Warnick cabin, Mr. Junkins saw that Landy's tracks veered off the path and into an open buckwheat field. There were no other tracks in the snow as Mr. Junkins followed his daughter's trail. Approximately twenty feet into the field, Lundy's tracks indicated that she had turned around several times and then simply disappeared. It was as if she had been plucked from the earth. There were no tracks of anything following her and no drag marks in the field. Landy's footprints simply vanished.

Mr. Junkins continued on to the Warnick cabin and inquired as to whether his daughter had been there. He learned that the child had never made it to the cabin. Mr. Warnick joined in the search, and the alarm was sounded. Many other men came out to help in the frantic search for the missing child. February days are short and the nights are bitterly cold in the West Virginia mountains. Everyone knew that Landy had to be found before nightfall.

Late that night, the search was suspended. The next day, an even larger group of men gathered to continue the search. But by the end of the second day, it was clear that Landy was not going to be found.

The men returned to the Junkins cabin and told Mrs. Junkins that her daughter was gone. The bereaved Mrs. Junkins went into an immediate depression. She neither ate nor slept, but just sat beside the fire and stared. Her state was precarious. Unfortunately, events over the next few weeks would only make matters worse.

Around February 4, a farmer named Hance Hardrick, who lived a few miles away in Rattlesnake Run, had his own experience. It had been a very cold winter, and Hance had brought his sheep in close to the house and built a bark shelter to protect them from the weather. When Hance went down to feed the sheep that afternoon, he found the sheep all cowering in one corner of the shelter. What's more, something large had ripped a hole through the roof of the shed. He quickly realized that one sheep was missing, and further examination of the hole showed that the animal had somehow been forced upward through the gaping hole. Hance realized that this had to have happened while he and his wife were in town earlier that day buying provisions.

Outside the shed, Hance looked for any tracks in the snow leading to or away from the shed. There were no tracks to be found, so where did the sheep go and how? Hance did not have any idea until a couple weeks later, when he read some amazing reports in the newspaper.

On February 7, Webster County Deputy Sheriff Rube Nihiser decided to take his adult son hunting. The two were looking for deer along the foot of Owl Head Mountain, when they picked up the tracks of a doe and her fawn. The pair tracked the animals across Piney Ridge and into some mountain laurel beds near Sugar Run. Rube knew that ahead of them was an open area where a fire had burned down the vegetation a while back. This area was part of a favorite deer path, and he was confident they'd soon sight the deer. Suddenly the two men heard terrible cries coming from the direction of the clearing.

They hurried forward to find the doe and her fawn being attacked by a giant bird. It flew upward and then swooped down to strike them with its nearly foot-long beak. The men had never seen anything like the beast, and they simply froze. The doe fought to protect her fawn, but it was a losing battle. In one last swoop, the huge bird grabbed up the fawn in its talons and flew off. The fawn bleated pitifully, and Rube regained his senses as the bird flew over him. He raised his gun and shot at it, but the bird didn't even flinch.

The two men hurried forward, but the doe seemed in shock and didn't run from them. She just stood there. When they got closer, they could see blood dripping from numerous wounds on her body. She apparently was badly injured, but the worst shock came when they got near her head. The bird had jabbed both of her eyes out with that horrible beak. Rube and his son were horrified by the damage that the bird had caused, and Rube shot the injured animal so that it wouldn't suffer.

Later the two men estimated that the bird was as big as a man, with a fifteen- to eighteen-foot wingspan. It was brown with a ruff around the neck, white on its wings, and a light underbelly. The bird flew toward Snaggle Tooth Knob on Owl Head Mountain. The knob was an area where two outcroppings of rock looked like a mouth with jutted-up rocks forming teeth. Viewed from a distance, it looked very much like a snaggle-toothed face. The area of Snaggle Tooth Knob was almost inaccessible. One would have to climb a sheer mountain face to get to it, and in winter, snow and ice were also factors.

On February 12, a hunter named Peter Swadley was taken to a doctor in Addison for injuries he had received when he was attacked by a giant bird while out bear hunting on Piney Ridge. Swadley later said he had been hunting when he came to a clearing. He heard a long scream, something like a panther, but not quite. He turned to look up to where the sound came from, and he saw a large feathered creature coming at him. The beast locked its talons on him and attempted to pick him up. The sharp talons tore through his coat and shirt and lacerated him. The beast simultaneously struck him hard on the head with its sharp beak. The blow stunned him, and he had a three-inch-long gash on his scalp where the flesh was gone. Swadley fought desperately for his life as he wrestled to get away from the bird and flung punches at the beast.

He shouted for help, and his hunting dog, Gunner, turned back and attempted to attack the bird. The bird caught the dog as it lunged and tore open its stomach. At that point, the bird let go of Swadley and fastened on the dog, which was still alive and whimpering when the bird took flight. Swadley was cut badly in several places from beak wounds, but he watched as his poor dog was taken away.

As soon as he could, Swadley stumbled down the mountainside to the cabin of a man he knew. He was bleeding profusely and could have bled to death if Abe Kitsmiller had not been home. Kitsmiller bound the wounds to the best of his ability and loaded Swadley onto a horse for the trip down the mountain. The entire area was shaken by the event, because Swadley insisted that the bird, which the local authorities called an eagle, was as large as a man and had a wingspan between fifteen and eighteen feet. The newspaper called the bird an eagle in all future reports, but to this day, no raptors in West Virginia territory have been known to grow as large as a man.

This was not the only time a big "eagle" was seen in the area of Owl Head Mountain. A few years later, there was a rash of sightings of two big birds in the Webster area. According to accounts, the birds attacked livestock throughout the winter. They seemed to stay near Snaggle Tooth Knob, and it was speculated that the knob was a good eyrie for them.

Giant "eagles" or other big birds have been seen off and on over the years throughout West Virginia and Pennsylvania, and giant owls have been reported in West Virginia. In 1978 in Wyoming County, people reported seeing a large bird that was silver-blue in color with a huge wingspan.

In the case of Landy Junkins, after the other bird sightings, people began to say that the giant bird living on Owl Head Mountain had carried the girl off. History does not record whether her parents believed the story, but they might have wondered what the last moments of their child's life were like if the great and terrible mythical bird had actually existed and stolen her away.

Northern
Panhandle

The Phantom Hobo

Moving to a new town always requires some adjustments, but it does not often require adjusting to a spirit that haunts the railroad bed just beyond your backyard. But for one family who moved to Colliers early in the twentieth century, such an adjustment was required.

One late summer evening, a man reportedly was sitting on his back porch taking in the evening air and just relaxing, when he saw a sight that distressed him. Beyond his backyard ran a railroad bed and a very active set of railroad tracks. As the man watched, an old hobo came into view. The fellow wore a ratty jacket and old patched pants, and he carried in his hand a brown paper bag. From time to time, the hobo lifted the paper bag and took a swig of whatever was in the bag. The man watched in disgust as the hobo made his way up the tracks.

The man on the porch instinctively looked down at his watch and saw that it was just past 9 PM He knew that a train ran along that track at precisely 9:15 PM every evening, and he could not help but think that the hobo had better hurry on his way if he did not want to encounter that train.

At that moment, the gentleman's wife came out to join him on the back porch, and she too saw the hobo lingering along the tracks. She sat down and mentioned to her husband that the hobo had better hurry along. She saw the fellow take a drink from his bottle and realized that he could very well be intoxicated. She turned back to her husband and inquired about the time. By now, both were beginning to worry that the hobo was in danger.

To their horror, the hobo sat down on one of the railroad tracks as if to rest. Immediately, the woman began to urge her husband to run down and tell the hobo that he had to get moving before the train hit him. Her husband needed little prodding, for he was already on his feet and hurrying across the porch.

As he ran down his yard, he began calling out for the hobo to move on. He shouted that the train would be coming soon, and as if in response to his call, he heard the whistle of the 9:15 train as it moved down the tracks. The hobo turned toward the man who was shouting at him, but he was either incapable of understanding or too drunk to respond.

The man picked up speed as he ran toward the hobo. The shrill cries of the train moving rapidly toward them spurred him on. The huge light of the fast-moving locomotive bore down on the hobo as he seemed to struggle to rise. The man from the house nearby stopped running. Air burned in his lungs and his side ached, but he did not notice either of those things as he waited for the train's imminent collision with the hobo. From his vantage point, he knew that he would see the entire impact. The man held his breath as the train bore down on the hobo. But in the last second before the expected collision, the hobo suddenly disappeared from sight. The man was left standing there staring at the 9:15 train and nothing else. It took a few seconds before he was able to move. As he finally walked back to the porch and his horror-stricken wife, he looked up at her and said, "Everything is okay, just calm down. I think that the hobo must have been a ghost."

Weeks later, when speaking with his landlord, the man mentioned the hobo on the railroad tracks. The landlord confirmed it for him, telling him that many years before, an old hobo had been harassed and driven from town because he was an undesirable sight in the pretty little town. Drunk, discouraged, and alone, the hobo walked along the railroad tracks, befuddled and confused. He sat down on the tracks to wait for a train to come by so that he might hitch a ride to a friendlier place. But the alcohol had taken its toll, and the hobo did not hear the train in time to react. By the time he was able to struggle to his feet, the train had struck him and he was killed instantly. Every year since that night, the hobo returned on the anniversary of his death to relive his horrible last moments on earth. To the best of the landlord's knowledge, no one had ever tried to stop the hobo from being struck by the train before.

The family lived in the house near the railroad tracks for many years, and they always made it a point to sit on the porch on the night of the anniversary of the hobo's death. They would watch for him, but never again did the hobo appear to relive his death. It is speculated that the haunting was ended because someone had finally cared enough to try to save the hobo's life. Perhaps all he had wanted all along was for someone to care, and he finally found that person when the man risked his own life running along the tracks to warn the hobo about the train.

The Haunted Penitentiary at Moundsville

As places designed to contain and punish evildoers, prisons are frightful places that seem to become imbued with the anger, pain, and suffering of those confined inside the walls. The West Virginia State Penitentiary was built in an area known as Moundsville in 1866. It was modeled after Joliet Prison in Illinois. In an ironic twist, the prison was built with the use of convict labor.

According to local lore, the prison was built over one of the large, mysterious mounds in the area, which had been created by the Adena Indians as burial mounds for their dead. Over the years, many of the mounds have been raided for artifacts, torn down to make way for modern structures, or otherwise desecrated. It would not be hard to believe that those spirits who were disturbed by the building of the prison would not look kindly on the structure.

In 1876, the prison was finally ready to house inmates. It was a large stone building that squatted like a Gothic fortress near where the little town of Moundsville was springing up. With battlements and turrets, it truly resembled a medieval castle. The prison looked down on the town, giving a feeling of unease to those who lived in its shadow below.

Moundsville featured a unique system for entering the cell areas. In 1894, a cage was added on the first floor. After the prisoners were searched, they were placed in this caged wheel, and it was turned so that the prisoners could not attempt a last-minute escape as they were led to their cells. The prisoner had only one small opening to go through, and a guard was waiting to escort him to his new abode, where he'd be locked in.

Prisons have a way of growing, and this one quickly found itself bursting at the seams. At one time three men slept in each of the five-by-seven-foot cells. In 1929, the prison doubled in size. The prison complex eventually encompassed twenty acres of ground and included the warden's residence and office, administration offices, visitors areas, laundry rooms, a chapel, and a boiler house. The Central Receiving Building was where prisoners first arrived. The Hole was used to punish prisoners who misbehaved. The Execution Chamber housed the electric chair, which was nicknamed Old Sparky. Later this was moved to the Death House. In the Solitary Confinement Unit, prisoners were kept alone to protect either themselves or others. It is said that many people were driven mad by the solitude of this area. Sensory deprivation and loneliness are known to have a debilitating effect, and there were several suicides here. Rat Row was where informants and witnesses were kept away from the general population for their own protection. The most deadly prisoners were housed in the North Hall. The North Wagon Gate was used to temporarily house both male and female inmates and at one time also was used for executions by hanging. A series of wooden trapdoors in the floor of the second floor bear mute testimony to their grisly use. A trapdoor would open, and the prisoner would dangle through the floor until pronounced dead.

A total of ninety-six men died by execution within the stone walls of this fortress. The first form of execution used at the prison was hanging, and eighty-four men were hanged within the facility. In 1951, the state adopted the more modern method of electrocution, and an electric chair was introduced to the Death Row facility. From 1951 to 1959, nine more men died by this method of execution. This was considered one of the most violent prisons in the nation at one time, and countless other men lost their lives through brutality and suicide here. There were several famous violent prison riots in which inmates held guards and staff members captive. Each of those events seemed to have left its mark on the structure.

In 1986, the West Virginia Supreme Court ruled that the five-by-seven foot cells constituted a form of cruel and unusual punishment for the inmates. The prison began an extensive renovation project, but it ended abruptly and the doors were closed in 1995. Most of the prisoners were removed to the Mount Olive Correctional Complex to finish out their sentences.

Perhaps the most famous person ever to do time in Moundsville was Charles Manson, who later shocked the world by orchestrating a series of murders in California that would be labeled the Helter Skelter murders. Manson was a young man when he spent time at Moundsville. After he was convicted for his part in the multiple murders in California, Manson asked to be moved back here, and for years he repeatedly made this request. His family was from the area, and he hoped to be closer so that he could receive visits from them.

There were several infamous murders within the prison. In the recreation area called the Sugar Shack, an Arian Nation leader named Jasper was stabbed to death during recreation time. Jasper's ghost is said to haunt the area and is the most vocal and aggressive spirit. In 1973, during a prison riot, three inmates were stabbed by other inmates, and one of them died. The prisoners then set fire to the prison while they were still in it. The hostages that they had taken were all rescued alive, and there was minimal damage to the prison. In 1986, another riot broke out, during which three inmates were killed. The guards who had been taken hostage were rescued during this riot too. That same year, two inmates who were leaders in the same motorcycle gang were killed during a gang dispute. A third victim of the attack survived. In 1987, two prisoners got into an altercation during their exercise period, and one struck the other with a barbell and killed him. The list of murders and attacks stretches back to the very beginning of the prison.

After the prison was shut down, the Moundsville Economic Development Council took out a twenty-five-year lease on the building, which was placed on the National Register of Historic Places and opened for educational tours. The facility also was used to train correctional officers. The prison began its current incarnation when it was featured on MTV's *FEAR* and caught the imagination of America. Since then, those hoping to experience the paranormal have made pilgrimages here. The curious and the ghost hunter alike have taken the opportunity to tour and spend time in what many have called one of the most haunted structures in the nation.

The staff who offer the tours and coordinate the overnight ghost hunts have many stories to tell of their time within the walls of Moundsville. One woman reported walking through a cold spot that caused her to shake with fear. She also witnessed a black shadowy person whom she took a picture of. Stories of encountering shadowy figures and hearing screams from the cells, doors clanging shut, and the sound of footsteps running along the stairs and hallways are common. Guests also report being locked in cells and having heavy prison doors suddenly slam in their faces. Some folks report being touched, pushed, or pulled. The voices recorded inside the facilities are truly terrifying. One tourist was videotaping the tour, and when she watched it later, she heard a long, low, terrified scream. She and her family were sure that they did not hear the scream at the time. The scream sounded like someone in great pain, and they never would have been able to ignore such a cry. The penitentiary at Moundsville seems to be host to every manner of haunting and is one of the state's most active sites of paranormal phenomena.

Monument Place

The life of Colonel Moses Shepherd and Lydia Boggs was actually a chronicle of the birth of a nation, and Mrs. Lydia lived through both the American Revolution and the Civil War. Her story has much to do with the haunting of her former home.

Moses Shepherd and Lydia Boggs first met as young people. Their fathers were both frontiersmen and public-spirited men. The young son of Colonel David Shepherd, Moses was about eight years old when his father moved the family to the Wheeling area. At the time, it was raw frontier land, and David set about building a plantation in the wilderness, with Moses by his side. David taught his son to run the mill, which was a necessary part of running the plantation. The Shepherd family also built Fort Shepherd to protect themselves and other local families.

When Moses was about seventeen years old, Indians attacked the plantation and burned both the fort and plantation to the ground. All that remained was the mill wheel, which the natives apparently spared because they liked to see the wheel turn.

Soon after the loss of Fort Shepherd, Colonel David Shepherd was ordered to command and defend Fort Henry. He took his entire family with him, including young Moses. There the family and the others in the fort faced a fierce attack from the natives, prompted by the British. It was an intense attack that turned into a true siege. The women at the fort fought as hard as the men to protect themselves and their loved ones. They made bullets, loaded guns, and shot if necessary. One young woman named Molly distinguished herself by lifting her skirts and filling them with cannon shot, bravely running from man to man to distribute the ammunition.

It was during the siege at Fort Henry that Moses first met Lydia. Her father, Captain John Boggs, was stationed at a nearby fort and was sent to aid the besieged Fort Henry. Lydia went where her father did, and she worked as hard as any woman within the walls of the little besieged fort. Petite of stature and delicately made, Lydia was a great beauty, but her claim to fame would always be her indomitable spirit. Her hands were roughened and burned by hot bullets as she loaded guns along with the other women and did whatever other task presented itself.

Moses Shepherd made trips to the plantation to oversee its rebuilding, and his family also rebuilt the fort but redesigned it to better protect themselves. Young Moses made several trips to Fort Catfish in Washington, Pennsylvania, where Captain Boggs was commander, and he often saw Lydia. During this time, young Moses joined the military and achieved the rank of colonel. He courted Lydia for some time before she agreed to marry him. He and Lydia eventually wed, and Moses set about building their family home on the site of the first Fort Shepherd. He and his petite wife made several expeditions into the frontier, but Lydia did not complain once. Though she looked delicate, she had the constitution of a bear, and nothing seemed to burden her. She was a partner in the running of the plantation, and many admired her keen mind. She had a love of life that seemed vast and encompassing.

The house that Moses built for Lydia was one of the finest in the nation. It was a large stone affair with a separate kitchen and slave quarters. Inside, it boasted a fine library, an elegant drawing room, and every amenity of the day. Called Stone Mansion at the time, it was a home that Lydia loved and cherished until her death.

Lydia and Moses made frequent trips to Washington, and they were friends with many of the men who ran the nation. A particular friend was Henry Clay, and with his help, they pushed to build a national road that would support transport of men and goods east and west. Running from Cumberland, Maryland, to St. Louis, Missouri, this road was the only route east and west until the railroad came along. It played an important part in opening up the western part of America to white settlement and trade and was the only road ever completely constructed by the U.S. government. Colonel Moses Shepherd and his wife were important players in conducting business in the nation, and men like Polk, Clay, Jefferson, and Jackson frequented Stone Mansion.

When Moses died in 1832, Lydia was bequeathed everything. She ran the plantation well and managed the vast assets that were left to her. She was even willed the slaves as her own personal possessions.

A year after her husband's death, Lydia met and married General Cruger, a member of Congress from New York, but she retained all rights to the personal and real property that her first husband had bequeathed her. Lydia was a vibrant woman who kept her hand in politics and was beloved for her style, eccentric behavior, and wisdom. She could recite American Revolutionary history through firsthand experience and remained clear, sharp, and articulate until her own death in 1867.

One of Lydia's eccentricities was that she kept two dresses from each year, keeping them hung up so that she could flip through them. She once explained that the dresses conjured up memories from bygone days, and she kept them so that she might be reminded of what they represented. She was well respected, and many people commented that it seemed as if Mrs. Lydia could never die. She loved life so much that no one could ever imagine her giving it up. But Mrs. Lydia eventually did die at the age of 101, having witnessed the American Revolution, the rise and fall of the slave system, and the Civil War, and having helped shape the nation. It was little wonder that many could not imagine Lydia ever leaving the earth and her beloved Stone Mansion behind.

But perhaps Mrs. Lydia did not leave her mansion or the earth. Starting shortly after her death, there have been stories that Lydia's petite form has been seen in various rooms throughout her former home. She seems to be going on about life just as she had before her death.

Today the mansion is called Monument Place, renamed by a former owner, Lucie Loring Milton. The new name has stuck, but the spirits that haunt this place are decidedly part of Lydia's time. The mansion is now public property, and former staff claim to have seen Mrs. Lydia throughout the house. Perhaps the most dramatic phenomenon is that late at night, people have heard the sounds of a ball in the ballroom on the second floor. When they hurried upstairs to investigate, the music and laughter suddenly stopped. Some say that for just a split second, they witnessed the ball before everything faded away.

Monument Place is a grand house, a shining example of Colonial America, and apparently still home to one very intelligent and lively lady whom many still affectionately call Mrs. Lydia.

Mountaineer Country

The Lady in Blue

Some tales of the paranormal seem to be easily explained, but what about stories where nothing makes sense? From Clarksburg there comes a story from the early twentieth century that has lingered because the mystery behind the haunting was never solved.

Late one cold winter evening, a young boy who was no more than ten or eleven years old was sent by his parents to run an errand. The family lived in a large, two-story house high up in the hills overlooking the river. From their home to the water's edge was approximately half a mile, but because of their situation on the hillside, they could clearly see the river.

That evening they sent their son out with little thought that he would encounter anything that would harm him. At the turn of the twentieth century, Clarksburg was not a dangerous place, and their son often ran errands for them. The boy was bundled warmly against the cold, but the wind had a way of chilling even the most warmly dressed person to the bone. His only thought was to complete his errand and return to the warmth of his snug home.

As the boy was returning home, he noticed a young woman walking toward him down the hill. In the light cast by the windows nearby, he saw that she was dressed in a light blue chiffon dress. The woman had neither a coat nor any other protection against the biting wind. The young boy was taken aback by the woman's condition as she approached him. He realized suddenly that not only was she dressed far too lightly for the winter weather, but she did not even have shoes on her feet. As she passed him, he turned back to watch her go by. He spoke to her, but she did not respond in any way.

The boy was more than a bit startled by the woman's condition and demeanor, and he decided that perhaps she needed help. Despite his own discomfort, he turned around and began to follow her as she walked toward the river. The wind seemed to try to push him back up the hill, but he fought it as he stumbled forward. The young woman before him seemed not to notice the wind or cold. The boy stayed well back in the shadows, although he could not have told anyone why.

To his dismay, the young woman did not even pause when she came to the river, but plunged in, walking slowly through the cold waters that enveloped her body. The boy watched as she walked out until the water was over her head. He waited for what seemed like an eternity, but was probably only minutes, for her to return, but she never did. For some reason, he did not feel a sense of urgency to get help. In fact, when he reached home, he was resolute that he would not speak of the matter.

The boy went to bed soon after he got home. He had spoken not one word about the lady in the blue chiffon dress. Throughout the night, he dreamed repeatedly of her face looking vacant as though she were in shock. In his dreams, he saw her passing by him again, and he saw her enter the cold black water over and over. Each time the water closed over her head, he startled himself awake.

By morning, the boy was convinced that he needed to tell someone what he had witnessed. He told his parents about his encounter with the woman in the blue chiffon dress. He explained to them how she had walked right into the river water and allowed it to swallow her up.

His parents did not believe the boy. They could not understand why he had not spoken of this matter the night before if it had been true. They told him he must have had a nightmare or imagined the story of the woman. He was an honest boy, so they did not accuse him of lying, but he knew they did not believe him.

Despite all that his parents told him, the boy still stuck to his tale about the woman in the blue dress. He knew that he had not dreamed her up, and that she had died in the water the night before. Frustrated, he gave up trying to convince his parents that he was telling the truth. He figured that later on someone would find the woman's body, and then they would believe him.

Shortly after the boy had finished telling his story, his little brother came running into the house calling out to his parents that he wanted to show them something. The little boy ran into the room where his older brother and parents sat, and they all stopped speaking to stare at the little fellow. In his hands, he held a long strip of light blue chiffon material. His mother picked it up and straightened it out so that they could all see that it had been a light shoulder wrap for a fancy blue evening gown.

Now they believed that the boy had not imagined the lady in the blue chiffon dress. The family contacted the authorities, and the boy told his tale once more. But there would be no resolution to the story. The police looked for the body of the woman in blue, but they found nothing. No story ever came to light about a woman being drowned or committing suicide in the river that winter. Perhaps the entire family would have forgotten the incident and marked it down to childish imagination if it had not been for that blue chiffon wrap that lay on the top shelf of their closet for many years.

The Grant Town Mine Specters

Miners are a special breed of people. They spend their days buried alive doing one of the deadliest jobs that was ever created. They claw through the earth to make money for others and scratch out enough of a living to provide for their own families. These men live their lives facing death, and West Virginia's history is scarred with many terrible mine disasters. Cave-ins and collapses, deadly gas, and accidents with equipment are all facts of life, and most miners know of at least one person who has died in the mines. It should be no surprise, then, that the state's southern coal country is riddled with ghostly tales from the coal beds beneath the earth.

Grant Town is located on the Paw Paw Creek in Marion County. Named for Robert Grant, the vice president of the Federal Coal and

Coke Company, it is home to one of the largest coal mines in the world. The people of Grant Town were hardworking and used to doing without. They were simple folks who brought with them their many heritages, as well as their superstitions and beliefs about ghosts. At one time, people from fourteen different nations were working in the mines.

Over the years, many miners have lost their lives within the confines of the Grant Town mines. The miners can give the names of the disasters, and many can name the miners who have died during their lifetimes. Still other miners have become repositories of the tales of paranormal events under the ground.

One of the stories they tell is of a young man who lost his father in a mine cave-in during the 1920s. Several other men also died in that collapse, and their bodies were found, but the boy's father was not. His mother was devastated not only by the death of her husband, but also because his body would not receive a proper burial.

On the morning after the collapse, the mine boss told the young man that he had to go back down into the mine or be fired. The young man was under incredible pressure. His father still lay below him somewhere in the twisted shafts, but he and his family needed the money that the mine provided. Reluctantly, the boy stepped into the cage that transported miners down into the shaft and went to work.

That day, the boy was distracted and skittish. Somehow he got separated when moving through the mine and couldn't find his crew. He stumbled forward in the darkness to where he thought they were, but he could not find them. Suddenly in one of the side shafts, he saw a faint light like that from a mining lamp, and he turned down the shaft. Farther and farther down the shaft he followed the light. He called out softly for the men to stop, but the light moved onward. The air grew thin and damp. He found himself pausing as his burning lungs drove him onward. Surely the light would lead him to good air, the companionship of the other men, and safety. At last he rounded a corner and saw the light ahead. It was a shaft of blue flame. In the shaft of light, he saw his father's face. The boy rushed forward, overcome by the vision. Just as he reached the light, his feet fell out from under him. He fell into a hole and hit something soft. The boy sat up and scrambled away from whatever he had landed on. The thin light from his miner's light illuminated the hole, and he was horrified to see that he had landed on his father's lost body.

The boy scurried from the hole and made it back up the mine shaft. He stumbled into his crew and told them about his grisly find. The body was retrieved and his father received a proper burial. The boy and the miners believed that the father had led his son to the body so that the family could have closure.

Working below ground caused the men to build a bond of trust. Each man was responsible not only for himself, but for his companions too. His actions could save lives or cost them.

Another story from deep within the mine shafts is that of a specter who once appeared to say good-bye to his friend. A big Russian man who was head and shoulders above the other men once came to the Grant Town mine to work. The other miners called him Big John because of his size, and they often laughed about the giant man who worked deep within the mines. Big John was a friendly sort who talked the whole time he worked. His chatter made the hours pass faster, so the men didn't complain. One fellow in particular liked to work with the big Russian. Big John's job was to blast loose the dirt to reveal veins of coal. His partner would add the blasting caps after Big John set the charges. One night, Big John was around a curve in a shaft setting a charge, when there was a terrible blast. His partner picked himself up as soon as he could and stumbled to where Big John had last been. He was horrified to see the corpse of his friend, and even more aghast to see that his friend's head had been severed by the blast.

The accident report stated that Big John had dropped a stick of dynamite that had caused the explosion. The incident was over for the mine company, but those who worked with Big John missed his cheerful banter. His old partner often thought that he heard Big John's voice, but it always faded away down the shafts, and he wrote it off as imagination.

Weeks after the death of Big John, his former partner stepped into the cage to ride it down into the shaft. He caught a blur of motion and looked up to see that he was no longer alone. Big John stood beside him, wearing the same clothes he had on the day of his death. The fellow was amazed to see that Big John had his head tucked under his arm. He stared in horror at the head, until it looked up at him and began to speak. Big John's voice filled the cage. The partner scrunched his eyes shut tight and pretended not to see or hear anything. When the cage opened up, the partner stepped out and didn't look back. He never saw his friend Big John again.

The story of Jim Tokash is perhaps one of the oddest tales within the mines of Grant Town. Jim operated a coal-cutting machine that sliced into the rock walls of the mines to find the veins of coal. Jim was a vain man who disregarded some of the safety rules of the mines. It was company policy that if a cutter struck a sulfur ball, a mass of compressed sulfur several times harder than rock, he should stop drilling and call a mine supervisor in. The compressed sulfur was dangerous to cut through, and it could be costly if men broke several drill bits.

Jim, however, figured that he could take care of the problem himself. He had often cut through sulfur balls and destroyed several drill bits doing so. His boss warned him that he'd be fired if he did it again, but Jim did not listen. The next time he struck a huge sulfur ball, rather than call his supervisor in, he again tried to cut through it himself. The bit got stuck, and he got off his machine to loosen it. The bit slipped in the rock and cut his hand off. The hand fell away, and no one thought to pick it up as they tried to help Jim out of the mine to get medical help.

Months later, Jim returned to the mine, but only as a helper. He would never be able to run the heavy equipment again. Instead, he helped the man who took his job. His replacement felt the same way that Jim had about calling in mine bosses for sulfur balls, and one day he struck one while Jim was in a little cleft in the side of the shaft getting a drink. Jim's replacement slammed into the compressed sulfur, and the impact caused a fault to splinter and the roof to cave in.

Jim was knocked unconscious and woke up to disaster. He was the lone survivor of the collapse. Dead bodies surrounded him, and worse yet was the fact that the route he had used to enter the area was now closed off by debris. He sat and waited for a few minutes, but he knew that time was precious. Complete blackness would surround him as soon as the carbide lamp on his helmet burned out. He had to find safety, but which way should he go? Some of the shafts would only carry him farther away from help, while others might take him to safety.

As he considered the possible paths, a faint white light glimmered in the distance. Jim decided that was the path to take. Only a carbide lamp made a soft light like that, and if there was light, there should also be help.

Jim followed the light and finally caught up to it. To his dismay, the glowing light was coming from the pallid form of a hand—not just any ghostly hand, but his own severed hand. Jim stared at the hand and knew for certain that it was his lost limb. The ring on the third finger of the left hand was his own wedding band.

The hand pointed toward a shaft, and Jim turned that way. He suddenly knew that he had to follow the ghostly hand as it pointed him along. Eventually he heard voices and saw light ahead. He ran forward and found himself in a working shaft with a crew. Jim collapsed and told them how he had followed his ghostly hand to them. The men thought that Jim had been hallucinating. He realized that no one would believe him, but later that night he returned to look for the lost hand. It was gone and he never saw it again, but he always believed that his hand had saved his life.

When the mines first opened, horses were used to drag the heavy carts and pull the buggies that carried the men. Many of the beasts also died in mine collapses and accidents. Most of the men grew attached to the horses, and they watched over the beasts and guarded them. For a man named Flora, though, the beasts would mean much more.

Flora filled coal cars for a living. He and his partner took turns leading the horse that pulled the car in his section back to the top. One night old Flora, an immigrant with a broken accent, noticed that his younger partner was struggling to keep up. When it was the younger man's turn to lead the wagon upward and dump it, Flora volunteered to take his turn and told the boy to rest.

As the man and horse worked their way slowly toward the top, the horse suddenly balked. Flora cursed the beast for being stubborn, but then he heard a sound from above that every miner dreaded—a long, low moan as the wooden ribs of the mine gave way. The earth tumbled down, along with broken timbers, and darkness swallowed the man and horse.

When Flora came to, he found that he and the horse were battered but not dead. He freed them both from the debris. He felt dazed,

and his head hurt terribly. He knew that the air was growing bad and he could not rest, but somehow he was too tired to move. Hours would go by before he was missed, and by then he could be dead.

In the darkness, he felt something nudge him and realized that it was the horse. Suddenly he began to question his own senses. The horse seemed to speak to him in a deep voice. "Get up," the beast coaxed. "Get up, Flora, and I'll lead you to safety." Flora knew that bad air could make men hallucinate, and he believed that was what was happening until he felt the horse push him over on his back. "Get up, Flora," it called out again. "I can lead us to safety, but you must hurry."

Flora struggled to his feet and held on to the horse's mane. The beast moved forward in the darkness slowly, and Flora stumbled along. Every so often he would moan, and the horse would stop to let him rest. Soon the air seemed better, and his lungs did not ache so badly. Flora never let go of the horse until he reached the bottom of the vertical shaft. He opened the cage, and the horse dragged the heavy coal wagon inside. Everyone thought that things were fine until Flora confided his story to a friend.

From that day on, Flora watched over his friend the horse. He cared for it, brought it treats, and made sure that the wagons were not too heavily filled. When the mine converted to mechanical transport, Flora quit the mines. He would not work without his friend the horse.

In another eerie story, a cage operator once had quite a scare in the south section of the Grant Town mine. He was working the night shift, and his job was to take men down into the mine and bring them back up. It was a fairly easy job, and often new men started out as cage operators. This operator had been working only a couple weeks when he had a strange experience. He was at the foot of the vertical shaft in his cage, waiting for someone to go up. In the distance, he saw two swinging red lanterns coming from a side shaft. Two men came to the cage carrying their lanterns. They looked tired and ragged. They stepped silently into the cage, and the operator worked the mechanism to make it move upward. The men bent to set their lanterns down on the floor. Light and shadow played across the cage as the machine moved upward. At the top, the operator pulled back the wire cage door to let the men step past him. No one moved out of the cage, so he turned back to see why the men had not moved. There was no one in the cage, but the two red lanterns were still sitting on the floor.

The cage operator later told his story to some friends, who asked him to show them the lanterns. The men had worked in the mines for years, and they recognized the lanterns as ones that were no longer used. They then asked the cage operator what shaft the men with the red lanterns had come from. He took them down and started down a shaft. The other men stopped him.

Topside once more, they told the young man that the shaft he indicated had been walled in after a terrible cave-in about six months earlier. Six men had died in the cave-in, and they still lay down there buried in the rubble. The shaft was unstable, and there was no way to get to them without dislodging the ribbing that was broken and causing a second cave-in. Furthermore, they informed him, the lanterns he had shown them had been used at the time of the mine collapse, but they had been replaced with other lanterns afterward. None of the red lanterns were left at the site.

The cage operator and the miners were left to wonder if two of the men buried in the cave-in had tried to leave their graves to return home. The cage operator vowed that he would no longer stay in the shaft if he ever again saw red lights swinging along the caved-in corridor.

The last story from the mines began in the darkness of a mine shaft but ended in a private home. During one of the many mining disasters in the Grant Town mines, a miner was decapitated. His body was laid to rest, and his widow was thrown out of her home because she no longer had anyone working in the mines. A neighborhood woman invited the poor lady to come and stay with her family. All the miners' wives knew that they faced eviction if something horrible befell their husbands, and they tried to band together, because they had no one but each other to lean on.

One evening the poor widow was sitting with her hostess in the living room, when there was a knock on the door. The lady of the house got up and answered the door. She let out a shrill little scream and stumbled backward.

The widow whirled around and saw a ghastly site. In the doorway was her husband, holding his own head in his outstretched hands. The widow was horror-stricken as she watched her headless husband walk through the living room and kitchen and out the backdoor. She and her hostess followed behind as he made his trek, and on the porch something made a slight tink. Two men working in a nearby yard also saw the headless specter. All four watched as he walked across the backyard and disappeared into the twilight.

The next day, the two women were on the back porch discussing what had happened. The hostess was sweeping while she talked. Suddenly she heard a little clatter on the board porch and looked down. There was a gold ring. She picked it up and handed it to the widow, who immediately recognized it as her husband's ring. It was what he had dropped on the previous night.

The wedding rings were the only valuable things the widow had owned. She had been dreading the fact that she would have to sell her own ring to buy a bus ticket to her parents' home. She could have kept her husband's ring, but she had chosen to bury it with him. Now he had returned it to her. She believed that he meant to tell her it was all right to sell the ring and go home now.

She did return to her family home and eventually remarried, but she never forgot the story of her first husband, who had died in a Grant Town mine accident. His last act of love and kindness stayed with her always.

The ghosts who haunted the mines of Grant Town were much like the men who worked there. They never seemed to cast blame or seek revenge, but just wanted to say their good-byes, right wrongs, or continue their work. They were simple, honest men in life, and it seems that even death has not stopped these resourceful men from completing their goals.

The Ogua Monster

When white men first set foot on the land that would become West Virginia, everything was a mystery to them. They saw the New World as a virgin bride for their taking, but nothing could be further from the truth. The land was old with traditions and the history of the native peoples with which this area was heavily populated.

As the white men settled in and took as their own the beautiful mountains, they listened to the natives at first. They looked down on the native people as primitive, however, and began to scoff at their traditions, history, and legends. They poked fun at the tales of giant hairy men who came and carried away their children or smaller hairy men that the natives called apple pickers because they came and gathered from the land just as the natives did. Near the Monongahela and Ohio rivers, the settlers first heard the stories of the Ogua.

The natives warned the newcomers to beware of the Ogua, who lived in the waters of those two great rivers. They said that the water beast hunted animals that came to the water's edge to drink, snatching at the hapless creatures and wrapping them in its mighty tail to drag them under and drown them. The Ogua also could carry off a man and drown him. They described the Ogua as a great beast with a long serpentine body, a stout set of jaws, and four small legs. But the very idea of a sea monster was laughable to the settlers.

All the local tribes warned the newcomers to beware of the beast. They always offered the monster a dead deer or other food so that they might cross the waters safely. The settlers saw this as a waste of fine food, but that was before they encountered the Ogua.

Soon isolated settlers began to have their own encounters. People going down to the water's edge to fill their buckets saw the beast. Others saw the creature as they boated or worked along the rivers. It soon became apparent to them that the Ogua was real.

Little more is known about the Ogua. Does the creature still exist? Perhaps in the waters of the Ohio and Monongahela rivers, there is a creature lurking that learned long ago to come out only along the uninhabited areas late at night to snatch up a deer and drag it back into the inky depths of the water. No sign would be left as the waters closed back over it to hide their secrets.

Dave Morgan's Dream

The Colonial period was perhaps the bloodiest in all of American history. A war without rules was fought that lasted for more than a hundred years. Neither side recognized the concept of avoiding civilian casualties, and mercy was rarely shown. The Indians fought for the survival of their race and way of life, and the white men fought to supplant the Indians in their own lands. In no other conflict in American history was it considered acceptable to murder innocent men, women, and children. Settlers who were peacefully assembled could wind up being tomahawked to death, their children kidnapped, and their homes burned without the slightest provocation. Peaceful

Indians could be murdered and their villages decimated in retaliation for acts that others had committed. No one paid attention to punishing the appropriate parties. This was a race war, and it made this the most dangerous and deadly period in American history.

In order for the frontier settlers to survive, they had to group together to protect each other. Armed parties of men stood guard on their neighbor's fields while they planted, worked, and harvested. Older children carried guns to protect their siblings on the journey to school. And near most settlements stood a fort or fortified house of some sort where the community could gather and protect themselves in times of danger.

Colonial America was dotted with forts to protect the first settlers. In West Virginia, between Prickett's Creek and Pawpaw, along the Monongahela River, sat Prickett's Fort. In times of trouble, the local settlers would gather at the small fort for shelter. If they had enough warning, they would bring their valuables and drive their livestock in with them, but all too often they had to flee without any possessions.

In the spring of 1779, David Morgan, his sixteen-year-old son Stephen, and his fourteen-year-old daughter Sarah were living at Prickett's Fort. They had been at the fort for several months because the Lenni-Lenape, Mingo, and Shawnee nations were conducting a series of raids along the Monongahela. Early on, several people had been killed and scalped, and Morgan had taken his family into the fort to protect them from becoming casualties in this never-ending war.

By spring, the raids had slowed to a trickle, and most of the frontier families were hoping to return home soon to plant their gardens and fields. They would need to sow grain if they were to survive for another year. David Morgan, like so many other homesteaders, began to worry about how and when he could return to his cabin. The commander of the fort finally announced that it would be safe for the farm families to go home, but Morgan had been sick for a couple weeks and was exhausted all the time, suffering from a fever probably brought on by confinement and bacteria in the water. So he instructed his son and daughter to go to the cabin without him to begin the spring work.

The young people set out cautiously to fulfill their father's request. Meanwhile, Morgan lay on the narrow rope bed in the quarters he had shared with his children and fell asleep. He began to dream of his children and his homestead. In his dream, he vividly saw his children finishing up their work clearing the garden.

Then, to his horror, he spotted movement in the trees just beyond the edge of the cabin site, and he strained to see what was moving there. Two Indians were watching his children as they worked. The Indians were dressed for battle, and their faces were painted in red and black. Morgan shouted to alert his children, but they did not seem to hear him. As they continue to work, the Indians crept closer and suddenly charged at the two children. He heard Sarah scream and saw Stephen fall beneath the blade of a tomahawk. The dream was too much for him, and Morgan was startled awake. For brief seconds, he lay in his bed trying to make sense of what he had just dreamed. It was the most vivid dream of his life, and somehow he knew he had to hurry. He struggled up, grabbed his gun, and took off as fast as he could through the woods toward his homestead.

As he came up the path toward the cabin, he saw that the children had begun to clear the family garden. Morgan stopped for a moment to catch his breath, and as he watched the children, he realized that he'd seen this scene before in his sleep. His eyes flew to where he remembered the Indians had been in his dream, and there they stood. Morgan stumbled forward as fast as his feet could take him. He was no longer a young man, and the illness had made him slower and weaker than he had ever been, but fear drove him on.

Just then the Indians slid past the edge of the tree line and darted toward his children. Morgan raised his gun. He shouted for his children to run to the fort, and in that moment the Indians turned toward him. They moved across the ground incredibly fast, but Morgan managed to get off one shot. One of the Indians collapsed onto the ground. The other continued toward Morgan with his tomahawk raised high, and Morgan was forced to drop his weapon and grab his own hatchet from his belt. The two men were locked in mortal combat. For a moment, Morgan believed that he would not be the victor, but in the end he threw off the younger man and caught him with a mighty blow. While the second Indian lay stunned and bleeding, Morgan grabbed his gun and ran after his children. Morgan knew that his only hope of survival was to make it to the fort before the young Indian recovered and caught up with him. He was not strong or young enough to win a second battle with the warrior.

Morgan's children met him at the gates of the fort, along with several armed men who were on their way out to help him. The exhausted man collapsed, and they carried him inside so that he could rest. When he eventually was able to speak, he told his children and the onlookers the entire story. For the rest of his life, David Morgan believed that God had given him a prophetic dream so that he could save his children's lives. It had been a beautiful spring afternoon, and if not for the dream, he would have had no reason to fear that anything was wrong.

The Lost Lovers

The beginning of the twentieth century brought with it a great many changes. Society's attitudes about independent young women working were beginning to change. The Civil War and the industrialization of the North had brought a great demand for jobs, and with so many young men locked in mortal combat, it fell to the women to fill those positions. After the war, women felt more capable and were not willing to give up their independence. No longer was it expected that every young woman would immediately marry and start her own family when she reached womanhood.

A certain young lady from Rowlesburg took a position on the domestic staff of one of the finer families of Pittsburgh. She was content with her job, but whenever she had the opportunity, she would ride the train back home to visit her family. One weekend while she was visiting home, she met a young man who intrigued her. The young woman made it a point to visit home as often as possible after that. The young couple began to court and soon fell in love.

Unfortunately, the young woman became pregnant, and her young gentleman had not yet asked her to marry him. In desperation, she went home and confessed to him that she was with child. She had thought that when she spoke to her lover, he would rescue her, but that was not what happened. Though the young man did love her, he panicked at the idea of suddenly finding himself a married man with a child, and he ran away. He knew that he was leaving the young woman alone to face the stigma of being unwed and with child, but in his own fear, he had no room for pity for her plight.

The young woman was horribly desperate. She knew that her job would soon end when her employers found out about her condition. She also knew that her family would be ashamed of her actions, and she had no idea what would become of her and the child.

For months, the young woman pretended that all was well while she worked, but at night she wept bitterly because her letters of entreaty to her lover went unanswered. She knew that soon the time would come when she must quit her job. At last the young woman knew she could no longer hide her condition, and she confessed to her family that she was with child. Her family was scandalized and refused to help her.

More desperate than ever, the young woman returned to work, but her employers had also discerned the state of affairs. She was confronted and dismissed.

The young woman boarded the train for Rowlesburg one last time. The rocking of the train made her nauseous, and her nerves were strung tight. All she could do was appeal to her family once more for help. The young woman stepped out on the platform to catch a breath of air and collect her thoughts. Below her she saw the Cheat River glide by, and in that moment despair overwhelmed her. The young woman leaped from the platform of the moving train to her death in the cold waters of the Cheat River far below.

When news of the young woman's death reached her lover, he was devastated. He knew that by abandoning her, he had left her in a position where she had no hope, and that was why she had jumped from the train. Remorse for his actions haunted the young man, and he knew that he too deserved death.

On the anniversary of the young woman's death, her lover disappeared. Weeks later, his body was found in the caves along the Cheat River near where she had jumped. The young man had drowned himself as well.

The following year, railroad workers witnessed the misty form of the young woman rise from the water on the anniversary of her death. As the men watched in horror, a second mist rose in the distance along the riverside and floated out to join the first mist. The two misty figures blended together and faded away. It is said that on the anniversary of their death, the young couple come together once more, reaffirming in death what they knew life—that they should have been together forever.

Eastern Panhandle

The Highway of Bones

During the Civil War, both the Union and the Confederate armies stomped across West Virginia many times. Some of the towns in the state passed back and forth between Union and Confederate control thirty, forty, or even more times. The people who lived there were suffering greatly. Both armies liberated food, forced the people to put them up, and destroyed their homes and livelihoods. Along the way, the great armies also littered the roads with their gear as well as their wounded and dead.

Many a body was found abandoned along the various roads that pass through the state, but the highway now known as Route 11 had more than its share of such tragedy. Route 11 was a major highway even during the era of the Civil War, and both armies used it constantly for travel. It was the only North-South route at that time, so it was a busy road. Along the length of it, battles and skirmishes were fought when groups of enemy soldiers collided.

As men died or grew too ill to be cared for, they were often abandoned along the highway. Dead bodies were buried by the road, and the injured that were slowing down the armies were left there too. The people of the area were left to deal with the aftermath of this destruction and devastation. It is said that for years after the war, graves littered the roadsides, and many an unknown soldier was unearthed during road improvement projects. Eventually the earth was washed away in some places, and the gray bones of the dead were uncovered.

Over the years, ghost stories sprang up along the length of the road. How could this unofficial burying ground not spawn ghostly tales? Route 11 has always been known as a dangerous road. It twists and turns through the mountains, and at night fog often shrouds it. It's no wonder this highway earned a ghostly reputation.

The stories of the spirits along the road are not well known, but some locals have had unnerving experiences. One ghost in particular has often been reported near the Martinsburg area. A local resident and folklore collector has heard several tales of sightings of spirits along the road near Spring Mills. One foggy night, a driver was terrified when a man in a Confederate cavalry officer's uniform rode out of the mist alongside the road. The driver jammed on his brakes as the horse and rider faded back into the mist.

On another occasion, a driver traveling along the road skidded to a stop when a man in Civil War clothes ran out in front of his car. The driver thought for sure that he had hit the man, but he had felt no impact. When he calmed down, he proceeded on his way. Later he saw a handprint on the front of his car. He believed that it came from the phantom soldier, who had held his hands out as if to stop the car from barreling down on him.

Is it possible that phantom soldiers are returning on misty, damp nights to ride forward into battle? Considering that so many Civil War battlefields seem to be haunted, who's to say that Route 11 is not equally haunted by those who died alongside the road during this nation's greatest conflict?

King's Daughters' Court

The beautiful, old, gray stone building immediately catches the eye of passersby. There is something arresting about the structure, and something haunting as well. It does not take much imagination to see ghosts looking from the windows, and perhaps ghosts do look out at the world from King's Daughters' Court, for it is said to be haunted.

King's Daughters' Court is actually an old hospital that has been shut down for many years. It was built in 1797 as the second prison for the town of Martinsburg. In 1890, an order of nurses was begun in the area. The women called themselves the King's Daughters, referring to serving their father, God the King. The nurses often cared for the ill prisoners, because they were not allowed to nurse many other people. Although Clara Barton had proven during the Civil War how beneficial nurses were to the ill and injured, many people still believed that nursing was best done at home. An area doctor named McSherry often worked with the nurses, and he grew close to them. He became friends with Sister Patricia, whom he called Sister Pat, and he listened as she often lamented that she and the other sisters could not start a real hospital because people did not want to be nursed by the women.

One day in 1890, Dr. McSherry was called to the train station to meet a train carrying a sick woman. The woman had gone into labor on board the train, and she and the new infant were doing poorly. Dr. McSherry quickly examined the poor woman and ordered that she and the baby be taken to the room at the prison where Sister Pat and the nurses worked. He sent word to Sister Pat that if she still wanted to start a hospital where the sisters could nurse people other than the prisoners, he was sending along her first two patients.

The sisters tended the woman and infant and saved them both from death. After that, the issue came up of building yet another prison. The prison where the sisters were working was over-crowded, and there were other concerns that needed to be addressed. Sister Pat realized that she was close to her dream. The nursing order purchased the building in 1893 for $2,610 and opened the building as a hospital on May 15, 1896, after it had been remodeled. The hospital of King's Daughters' Court came into being.

In 1913, the Sisters applied for and were granted a charter to begin a nursing school in the old prison building, which would be used to train nurses. During that time, 444 nurses graduated from the school. Among them was Margaret Beard, who died in 1918 while nursing the wounded in Europe during World War I.

The hospital eventually shut down in 1973, and then the building was used as office space and for various other purposes. At some point, the structure was gutted. The native limestone shell survived, but the flooring for all three floors was completely destroyed. There is little doubt that many lives were lost in the

structure over the years, but the most common story associated with the building is not of a person who died inside the hospital. In fact, this is a most unusual haunting, because this ghost seems to seek out only travelers through town and has never been known to appear to anyone who lives there.

According to a local source, on several occasions people passing through Martinsburg late on a summer evening have seen a little girl walking along a highway. The fact that the child is out late at night always causes concern for the travelers, who stop to offer the little girl a ride. The girl seems distraught and tells them that she must get to the hospital, where her mother is. The traveling good Samaritans offer the little girl a ride. She gets into their car and directs them back into town toward the large, gray building in the old part of the city.

The little girl gets out and runs up to the front door of the hospital as the travelers watch. There are lights on throughout the building, and a nurse in an old-style uniform hurries out to greet the child. The nurse ushers the child inside, and the travelers resume their journey, feeling that they have helped the little girl.

On occasion, the helpful travelers have returned through Martinsburg and have driven back past the old, gray building. To their great surprise, it now looks abandoned. Further inquiries only prove to unnerve them even more, when they learn that the hospital has been shut down for many years, and no one could have been in the building the night they drove the child to the hospital.

There are many mysteries about this little ghost tale. Who were the child and her mother, and why does the little girl haunt the roadside and hospital? These are mysteries that no one has been able to answer. There is a scrap of a legend that claims that in the early 1900s, a woman who worked at the hospital often had to leave her seven- or eight-year-old daughter alone at home. One night, it is said, the child attempted to find her way to the hospital because she was upset and sick. While walking along the road where she is seen today, she disappeared from the roadside. No one ever learned what became of the little girl, and her mother eventually died from the pain of the loss of her child.

Another story has it that one of the Sisters jumped from a third-story window in the building. The young nurse was a black woman who had fallen in love with a white male patient. He returned her feelings, but they both knew that they could never act on their emotions. In despair, the nurse was said to have climbed to the top floor of the building and jumped. She died just outside the structure, and it is said that her scream and the thud of a body have been heard directly below the center window of the building.

A ghost tour recently began in Martinsburg, and shortly afterward, people began to contact the tour guides with stories about hauntings in this town. One woman confided to them that several years earlier, when the hospital building was abandoned, she was driving past it when she caught sight of a woman in a red cape at a top-floor window in the front of the building. As the driver slowed down, she saw the woman throw herself from the window. Another driver behind her had also witnessed the events, and horrified, both drivers pulled over. The women summoned the police, but they were shocked to find out that there was no body and no reason to suspect that anyone had jumped from the building. Until that night, neither woman had ever heard about the ghostly nun who supposedly had died there.

King's Daughters' Court is currently being renovated and is awaiting a new lease on life. Whatever it becomes in its new incarnation, it will carry a unique history and likely a couple of interesting and unusual ghosts.

The Restless Spirits of Harpers Ferry

Harpers Ferry is a little town nestled on the side of the mountain along the banks of the Potomac and Shenandoah rivers. It seemed a town destined to be famous from the very beginning. In 1761, Thomas Jefferson observed "the passage of the Patowmac through the Blue Ridge." He stood on a rock that today is called Jefferson Rock and is a site that thousands visit every year.

George Washington also spent time in Harpers Ferry because he was president of the Patowmac Company, which was charged with improving water transportation. In 1794, Washington proposed that the government locate their new armory at Harpers Ferry—the same armory that John Brown later attempted to take over. In a strange twist of irony, one of the more than sixty prisoners John Brown took in Harpers Ferry on the night he began his raid was a great-great-nephew of George Washington named Colonel Lewis Washington.

The first known haunting of Harpers Ferry might be that of the Phantom Army. This area saw action not only in the Civil War, but also just after the Revolutionary War as well. In 1798, France was threatening to attack the fledgling nation, and General Pinkney was stationed at Harpers Ferry. His men set up camp on a ridge above what is now High Street. The place is still called Camp Hill because of that event.

Nothing much happened, so General Pinkney marched his men to keep them in shape. The men stomped down the hill each day as the drums and fife played. But then cholera began to ravage the troops, and men grew ill and collapsed. Soon the bodies began to mount up, and they were buried on the west bank of Camp Hill. Many men never left Camp Hill that terrible summer.

Over the years, the people of Harpers Ferry have reportedly experienced the haunting of Camp Hill many times. They tell of hearing what sounds like a parade coming. First the drums catch their attention, and then the lute cuts in sweetly. The sound of marching feet tells them that a large group is coming through. They rush outside to see who is passing by, only to find that there is nothing to see. The sounds eventually get closer, until they are sure they should be seeing the marchers, yet no one appears. They finally hear the marchers moving along past them, but still they see nothing. The marching and music fade out in the distance, and the phantom procession moves along, but not a soul has been seen. The first time the Phantom Army is encountered, it is terrifying, but soon people grow used to hearing the men eternally marching down the street.

Harpers Ferry was a little town tucked on the hillside along the Blue Ridge Mountains when it came to the attention of abolitionist John Brown. Brown has been described variously as a zealot, hero, crazy man, and visionary. The fact is that he was probably a little bit of all those things.

John Brown did not start out to be a rebel or zealot. He married Dianthe Lusk and became a family man. Settling in Meadville, Pennsylvania, he began a successful tannery. He also started a little church because there was not one close by and opened a post office. He was always an ardent abolitionist and became part of the Underground Railroad. A secret room was built in his tannery, where he often hid slaves. He was known locally as a humble, honest man who worked hard and lived his beliefs. Most of the area respected him, and he prospered, but then bad luck began to plague John Brown.

Brown's wife died giving birth to his seventh child. He subsequently married a sixteen-year-old girl named Mary May, and together they had thirteen children. The tannery began to fail, the good lumber from the Brown farm had already been logged off, and money became an issue. Brown found himself facing bankruptcy with twenty children to care for. He also felt the weight of losing the tannery and having to let go the fifteen men who had worked for him.

In a bid to restart his life, Brown moved the family to Ohio in 1835. He struggled but was never able to recapture his good fortune once more. He followed several of his sons to Kansas, where one was killed in a border war raid.

Brown was a man filled with righteous indignation and the will to do something about it. He did not believe that slavery would end without drastic action, so he began to put together an army to invade the South. His opening salvo would be to capture the arsenal at Harpers Ferry.

Brown did succeed in his objective of capturing the Federal Arsenal on the night of October 16, 1859, but after that things went badly for him. He had overlooked some weapons in a distant building, and the local men got hold of them. The men picked a high vantage point and began to barrage the arsenal buildings with gunfire. Men were injured and killed. Brown and the remainder of his men were driven into the engine house. Brown and several men were captured. Other rebels were shot or captured nearby, and one slave was drowned.

John Brown had been so consumed by his hatred of slavery that he became nearsighted. He had not truly thought out what he would do if the raid worked. He had hoped that the local slaves would mutiny and join him. Then they would move from place to place, causing uprisings and building up an army of freed blacks. But in reality, just a few slaves revolted and joined Brown, and they brought with them only the crudest homemade weapons. His dream of a massive slave revolt was doomed to failure.

Brown was hanged in December 1859 at Charles Town. He had succeeded in doing what he had set out to do, beginning a war that would eventually free the slaves. Abolitionists were outraged and began to work harder. The rift between slaveowners and the abolitionists grew wider, and within two years, the Civil War was raging. The death of John Brown had served to help him reach his objective.

In Harpers Ferry, people have claimed to see an elderly man with a big, bushy beard dressed in Civil War–era clothing walking the streets. A little brown dog accompanies the man. As they watch the fellow, he turns and heads down the hill toward the railroad beds and the former Federal Arsenal. The man meanders toward the engine house, and then to their astonishment, he walks through a wall and disappears. They have just witnessed what is said to be John Brown's ghostly evening walk.

Over the years, some very confused tourists have contacted the National Park Service about their sightings. They told an incredible tale that would have been hard to believe if it had not been heard before. The tourists insisted that they had been walking around Harpers Ferry and spied a man in period costume who looked amazingly like John Brown. They stopped the man and asked him to pose for a picture with them. The man always kindly did pose, but later when the film was developed, they were alone in the shot. No kindly old man dressed like John Brown ever appeared in the shots.

John Brown had visited Harpers Ferry several times while planning the attack. He often strolled around the town as if enjoying the weather, but what he really was doing was reconnoitering the area before his ill-fated attack.

The ghostly John Brown seems unconcerned and happy as he and the little dog stroll along. Is John Brown reliving the days just before the attack, or is he basking in the knowledge that he had begun the fight that would end slavery? The fact that he enters the engine house leads some people to speculate that Brown's ghost was there because of the raid, but it doesn't really matter to those who encounter his ghostly presence. They simply know that John Brown has not left Harpers Ferry yet.

John Brown and several of his men also were encountered outside the old engine house several years ago. According to the account, a man named Brad Matthews was visiting his hometown of Harpers Ferry, and late one evening, he was wandering the sites that he had seen so often as a child. One nice thing about a historic site is that things rarely change there. Matthews was standing behind the old engine house, looking out into the brush where he and his buddies had crawled as children, when his reverie was broken by what sounded like gun blasts. He slammed his body against the brick of the old engine house and jerked his head upward to see where the shots had come from so that he could head in the opposite direction. He saw no one but heard voices inside the building, so he sidestepped to the nearest window and peeked inside. Suddenly he froze. Someone was close beside him. "Don't you know that you shouldn't speak to the prisoners?" the voice demanded. Matthews looked toward the voice and was astounded to see three white men and two black men standing near him. All held old-fashioned weapons, but what amazed him was one of the white men, an old, lean fellow with a long, bushy beard and penetrating eyes. The man was a dead ringer for John Brown.

These were crazy reenactors, Matthews thought. "I'll talk if I want to," he said. One of the black men grabbed a gun out of his pants waistband and pointed it at Matthews. It occurred to him that these nuts might have real weapons.

The old man eased the gun down away from Matthews. "Easy now," he counseled his comrade. "I want to talk to this fellow." The old man pinned Matthews with dark eyes. "Do you own slaves, son?" His voice commanded the truth.

"Slaves?" Matthews stammered. He wanted to tell the guy he was a nut, but something about the old man's demeanor warned him not to say a word.

The old man reached out to grab Matthews, but he twisted away. Compelled by a sudden feeling that he had to get out of there, he dashed around the building and sprinted up the hill into town.

Behind him, guns discharged, and the old man bellowed at him. Matthews did not stop. Out of nowhere, a woman sudden rushed by him. "Don't shoot!" she screamed back to the men by the engine house. "Don't shoot him!" She blocked the shots with her body as Matthews ran up an alley. He turned back, but the woman was gone. Below him, he saw the dark figure of the old man watching him. Suddenly the old man turned, waved his arm, and headed for the woods. The other men fell in behind him.

Matthews went home and tried to calm down. As he rested, he realized the date. It was October 16, the anniversary of the night John Brown had commenced his deadly raid. It didn't matter to

Matthews if anyone else ever believed him. He knew with absolute certainly that he had met John Brown and some of his men reliving the events of that night.

In a sad twist of fate, the first one of John Brown's men to fall was a free black man named Dangerfield Newby. Newby's death was a tragic ending to a love story and a horrific part of the Harpers Ferry events that most people never hear.

Newby was a mulatto born from a union between a slave woman and her master. He was freed when his father moved the family to Ohio, which was a free state. But Newby was forced to leave behind in Virginia his wife and seven children, who were not freed slaves. His anguish over this drove the decisions he made for the rest of his life.

Dangerfield Newby made a deal with the man who owned his family to purchase his wife and the youngest child for $1,500. It was an incredible amount of money for Newby, but he set about earning it. He set up shop in Ohio at his trade of blacksmithing and worked himself ragged trying to save the money. He finally did manage to save up the required amount and made the trip to Warrenton, Virginia, to buy back his wife and youngest child. But his hopes were dashed when their master informed him that the price had gone up.

Newby saw no legal way to get his family back, but when he met John Brown, his hope was reborn. If the slaves revolted and freedom came to them all, he would have not just his wife and one child, but all of his family together again. It was an irresistible dream for Dangerfield Newby.

Although the Federal Arsenal housed guns in twenty-two buildings on the complex, there was little ammunition to be found. The citizen militia often cobbled up bullets from whatever they found at hand that could be shot through the barrel of a gun. One of the militiamen was firing six-inch spikes from his gun, and one of those spikes caught Newby in the neck and killed him.

After the battle, the militiamen savaged Newby's body, shooting it full of shells, stabbing it repeatedly, and then dragging it into a nearby alley, where it lay until some wandering pigs found it. Though the first pig that sniffed it ran off squealing, the rest of the herd devoured the poor man's corpse within minutes. Citizens of the town looked on and did nothing. There was no compassion for the man, even in death. He never received a Christian burial, but eventually his bloody, ragged clothing was gathered up, and a letter was found in it. The letter was from his wife and explained to everyone why Newby had taken the desperate chance, even though he was already a free man.

Dear Husband,

I want you to buy me as soon as possible, for if you do not get me somebody else will. The servants are very disagreeable; they do all they can to set my mistress against me. Dear Husband . . . the last Two years have been like a troubled dream to me. It is said Master is in want of money. If so, I know not what time he may sell me, and then all my bright hopes of the future are blasted, for there has been one bright hope to cheer me in all my troubles, that is to be with you, for if I thought I should never see you, this earth would have no charms for me. Do all you can for me, which I have no doubt you will. I want to see you so much . . .

Harriet Newby

The letter explained Dangerfield Newby's frame of mind and also explains why his spirit apparently cannot rest. To this day, the area where Newby's mutilated body was dumped is known as Hog Alley. Ever since Newby's horrible death, people have claimed to see a big black man in baggy clothes and a slouch-brimmed hat standing or walking through Hog Alley. When folks approach nearer, they always report seeing a terrible gash across the man's throat.

It is said that Dangerfield Newby haunts the alley because he never was able to free his family from the bonds of slavery. How ironic that he died participating in the one act that would spur the Civil War but never learned that his actions helped free not only his family, but many other slaves.

In 1833, the railroad linked Harpers Ferry with the more populated East and allowed the Federal Armory to be located in the small town. The tracks were laid through the armory yard. Beyond the yard near the river were warehouses that were soon abandoned after the armory opened.

Through the years, the shambling old buildings became home to transients and the homeless. During the late 1830s, a young girl named Jenny took up unofficial residence in one of the buildings near the train tracks. The old buildings were made of plain pine boards and had no insulation. In winter, the cold and wind seeped in. Heating the building was out of the question, but many vagrants tried to gather wood and made fires in crude fire pits they had made and in the fireplaces built into the warehouses.

One bitterly cold winter night, young Jenny was freezing to death. Her ragged clothing was no match for the howling winds and biting cold, and she huddled as close to the fire as she could. The meager heat helped alleviate the terrible numbness.

Suddenly Jenny's dress caught fire. The girl panicked and ran for the door. Her movements fanned the flames, and within seconds the young girl was a ball of fire. As she ran down the railroad tracks nearby, screaming in mortal pain, the railroad engineers saw the terrible sight, but by the time they caught up to the girl, there was nothing they could do.

Then their horror grew even worse. Coming through was a train moving fast. The train never had time to slow down before it struck and killed poor Jenny.

Ever since that terrible winter night, people have clamed to see a fireball or a woman on fire running up the railroad tracks screaming. Engineers often have reported the terrible sight of Screaming Jenny, as they call her, late at night. She runs along the tracks until her fire winks out where she was struck by a train and put out of her misery.

The Civil War spawned many of the ghosts of Harpers Ferry. No story is sadder than that of the little phantom drummer boy. The Town House in Harpers Ferry was used to house Union troops during the Civil War, and it was the scene of a singular act of brutality. The men who lived there captured a little Confederate drummer boy who was no more than nine or ten years old. At first the men kept the child with them to protect him from the brutal prison camps. Many men did not make it through those camps, and the child surely would have died. But they soon turned the child into their lackey, making him clean, polish boots, fetch food, and do their laundry. Worse yet, they became physically abusive to him as the war progressed.

At times the abuse was more than the child could bear, and he'd weep and beg them to let him return to his mother. This angered the men, who thought he was being ungrateful.

One day the Union soldiers were drinking and became particularly harsh with the child, abusing him both physically and ver-

bally. The child collapsed and began to cry. He pleaded once more to be allowed to see his mother. The soldiers were enraged. They grabbed up the ungrateful little bugger and tossed him back and forth while the child cried out in fear. One of the men tossed him toward a comrade standing beside the window. The toss was wild because of the thrashing child and the alcohol that clouded the man's judgment. The little boy crashed through the window and smacked into the pavement below. He was dead.

Ever since then, people have heard a child crying pitifully and a thin little boy's voice begging to be allowed to go home and see his mother. Sadly, even death did not free the little drummer boy from his tortured existence.

Looking down over Harpers Ferry and making an imposing sentry over the little town is the beautiful old St. Peters Catholic Church, built in 1833 from native stone in a neo-Gothic style. Inside the church, wide aisles give way to the original hard wooden benches that lead up to the altar made of carved Carrara marble. Jeweled sunlight falls into the sanctuary from the Tiffany stained-glass windows. The entire effect is inspiring.

Outside, an old cemetery twists down the hillside. Stone steps run the length of it, and the effect is humbling. It is easy to see why this church has been kept pristine since it was first built.

The story of this church is one of love, devotion, and faith. During the Civil War, it was tended by Father Costello, who refused to abandon his church, unlike so many other ministers. Each time the fighting drew close, he ran a British flag up the flagpole. Many times the town was shelled from an area called Maryland Heights, and the British flag was quickly sent flapping in the breeze. Neither side ever attacked the church, because they did not want to cause an international incident. That was part of the reason why St. Peters was the only church left standing in Harpers Ferry at the end of the Civil War.

Perhaps the church was also left unmolested because of Father Costello's acts of kindness. Boards were stretched across the pews, and the battlefield injured were brought inside. Within the church, there was no North or South. All men were cared for according to their need. Father Costello tirelessly changed bandages, cleaned bullet and bayonet wounds, and held cups to the dry lips of the men in his charge. At one time it was estimated that he had at least a hundred wounded men in his care. He did all he could for the men, and when some of them died, he prayed over them and arranged for their burial too. Word of his kindness spread as the injured were allowed to leave.

Two ghosts are believed to be associated with the church. One is the spirit of a young Catholic man who was brought to the church wounded after a battle. Father Costello laid the men in the church-yard and tried to tend the most severe wounds first. As he did so, the men were carried in and laid on the benches. The young Catholic man was comforted by the fact that he had been brought to a Catholic church. Here, he believed, he would be safe.

Father Costello passed over the boy again and again, because his wounds did not look that bad. What he did not know was that internally the young man was bleeding to death.

By evening, the young man was very weak. Still, he clung to his faith and was relieved to feel his stretcher lifted up. As he was brought into the church, he whispered faintly, "Thank God, I'm saved," and then drew his last breath. Perhaps the boy really was saved in a very different way than he had anticipated.

Since that event, people have claimed to see a golden glow com-ing from the doorway of the church. As they look at the glow and try to figure out what is making it, they hear a soft voice whisper, "Thank God, I'm saved," as the spirit of the young man relives his last moments of faith.

It should come as no surprise that Father Costello is also still tending his church. People often report that at 6 PM, the priest has been seen in his black robes and friar's hat hurrying from the rec-tory. Unless the people know the tale of Father Costello, they usu-ally speak to the unusually dressed priest, who never seems to notice them but hurries onward. He turns toward the church and walks through a wall. Witnesses are left shocked and puzzled. When they ask around town, there are plenty of folks to tell them that they just met the spirit of Father Costello as he hurries through a doorway that was closed up during the renovations after the Civil War.

Other people have seen the priest walking down the stairs through the cemetery at twilight. Perhaps he is praying for those he tended, or maybe he is just going into town for supplies. He never deviates from his mission and never speaks. In death, he is still showing dedication to his parish and the people of Harpers Ferry.

Harpers Ferry has many ghostly tales to tell, but not all of them are well known. Even the most casual of inquiries can elicit ghost stories in this town. At a local restaurant, the owner told of her own ghostly experience. She had once owned another restaurant on Main Street next door to the place she now runs. When she first moved into the other restaurant, she noticed a handprint on the wall. She tried to scrub it off, but scrubbing did not have any impact on the handprint.

She also noticed that she always felt watched while working alone in the building before and after hours. She was a pragmatic woman, and the feeling did not bother her. She simply noted it and kept working.

As the restaurant prospered, she decided to paint the dining room. That, she thought, would take care of the handprint. She painted over it several times, but it always bled through the paint. Now the woman was puzzled by the persistent handprint. She questioned the former owner but learned little. She was simply told that old buildings have their quirks, and she agreed with that.

At last the lady decided that the only way to get rid of the print was to cover it up. She found a painting that she liked and hung it over the handprint. She was not very surprised when she came in early in the morning on a few occasions to find the painting sitting on the floor turned to the wall below the handprint. Whoever the spirit was in the building, it seemed determined to let people see the handprint. The restaurateur never minded sharing her business with a ghost. She simply would rehang the painting for the day, and then remove it to please the spirit before leaving each night.

Harpers Ferry bears the marks of time. The history of the town is still very much in evidence, and so are the ghosts. It was a place of great passion and cruelty, and those emotions seem to come alive with the spirits who remain there.

Wizard's Clip

In the annals of ghostly phenomena, there is no subject more mysterious than the poltergeist. Traditionally, the word *poltergeist* means "noisy spirit." It was believed at one time that the poltergeist phenomenon was an extreme manifestation of a haunting.

Today most parapsychologists offer a very different definition. They say that the poltergeist phenomenon is actually an unconscious release of physical energy by a human being, and that in almost every instance it is associated with a person in puberty. Occasionally there are stories, though, that do not necessarily fit within the new definition. A case in point would be that of Adam Livingston and the Wizard's Clip. One of the things that make this story unique is that it was so well documented at the time.

John Adam Livingston was born in Lancaster County, Pennsylvania, in February 1739. When he was thirty-three years old, he inherited his father's farm in Smithfield, Virginia (later West Virginia), and moved his family to the 350-acre farm near Smithfield in 1772. There is a bit of controversy about the next bit of the story, but the traditional version states that one evening, Livingston and his family found a stranger on their doorstep. The man was very ill and begged them for a place to sleep. Livingston and the family took the man in, gave him food, and fixed him a bed near the warm fire. During the night, Livingston awoke when he heard the stranger's labored breathing and harsh coughing downstairs. Supposedly, Livingston went downstairs to tend to the stranger and found the man near death. The stranger begged Livingston to go get a priest so that he might be given the last rites. Livingston was a good Lutheran, however, and would not have a Catholic priest in his home. He tended to the man as best he could but refused to give the man the religious help he begged for.

By morning, the stranger was dead, and Livingston summoned several neighbors to come help him bury the body. They dug a hole in the corner of the Livingston property and interred the poor wayfarer. They offered him a good Christian burial and placed a wooden cross above his head.

Several days after the man was buried, Livingston awoke to the sounds of bells clanging in his bedroom. He heard dishes tumbling out of the cabinet downstairs and was sure that someone was either playing a practical joke or attempting to destroy the house. Over the next several days, Livingston quickly learned that no human being was playing a practical joke on him. Items flew about the house on their own, livestock disappeared, strange cries and screams came from the air, phantom bells rang, money disappeared, lanterns blew themselves out, fires popped up and disappeared at will, and dishes flung themselves across the room to smash into walls.

Not only did this ghostly presence terrorize him and his family inside the house, but it even extended outward to the entire property and beyond. The livestock suffered strange cuts, and animals disappeared from the barn.

One afternoon, Livingston came upon a wagon teamster sitting in the middle of the main road. When he approached the man and asked him what he was waiting for, the teamster cursed him out and told him to take down the rope that was stretched across the road. Livingston saw no such rope, but the teamster was adamant that it was there. Livingston again tried to reassure the man that he had not roped off the highway, but the teamster picked up a whip and flicked it at the rope. To the amazement of the teamster, the whip went straight through the rope as though it were not even there. More than a little upset, the teamster was persuaded to drive his wagon through the phantom rope. Throughout the day, Livingston was plagued by people who claimed to see a phantom rope that stopped them in front of his farm.

Within weeks of the phenomena beginning, Livingston's family faced the worst of the haunting. They began to hear the metallic click of large shears snapping open and shut. Any item on the farm was not safe from the phantom shears. Clothing, bedding, leather goods, books, and paper—all fell beneath the ghostly snippers. A woman who came to visit the family took off her good black bonnet, hid it inside her handkerchief, and tucked the packet into her pocket. Throughout her visit, she heard steady snapping sounds as though the clippers were at work, but no one could find anything damaged or destroyed. When the good woman left the Livingston home, she retrieved her bonnet from the safe abode in her pocket, only to find that it had been clipped to ribbons without her even feeling it.

On another occasion, a tailor came to visit the Livingstons. The tailor was on his way to deliver a suit to a neighbor down the road, when he heard about the ghostly phenomena. The tailor was determined that he would solve their problem straightaway. He was sure that the entire thing was a hoax being perpetrated either by the Livingstons themselves or a neighbor. While the tailor was in the house speaking with Mr. Livingston, the sound of shears clipping went on. The man did not solve the mystery, but he promised to return after he had delivered the suit. But when the tailor took the suit out of the paper parcel he carried it in, he found that it had been cut into small pieces inside the unmarked paper parcel.

Livingston begged his Lutheran minister to come to the house and pray, but it did little good. He then contacted an Episcopalian minister and three Methodist ministers, who also came to his house but were unable to help.

One night Livingston had a dream in which he saw a man of God in long robes, and a voice said to him that this man could help him. When Livingston awoke, he confided to a neighbor, Mrs. Richard McSherry, about his dream. Mrs. McSherry said that the only religious man she knew of who wore robes was a Catholic priest. She also told him that although there were no priests in the area on a regular basis, a priest would be in Shepherdstown the following Sunday to offer Mass. Despite his misgivings about Catholics, Livingston decided to attend the Mass. To his amazement, the priest who officiated at the Mass in Shepherdstown was the very man he had dreamed of. The priest's name was Father Cahill.

Livingston explained the situation to the Father and begged him for help, but Father Cahill was not sure that he should go to the Livingston farm. He was finally convinced by the McSherrys and other neighbors that Livingston was telling the truth and agreed to help.

On his first trip to the Livingston farm, Father Cahill sprinkled holy water in every room of the house and said a prayer. As he finished in the family room, a satchel of money suddenly appeared in the air and dropped in the doorway. Livingston informed Father Cahill that this money had been missing for months and thanked the priest for his help. The Livingston family hoped that this strange haunting was over, and for few days it seemed as though it was. But soon enough, the clipping of the shears resumed and all the other bizarre phenomena came back with a vengeance.

Livingston sent word to Father Cahill that the spirit had returned and begged him to give his family peace. Father Cahill had to apply to his diocese for permission to perform an exorcism, and the bishop contacted Father Gallitzin, a former Russian prince who had become a Catholic priest only two years earlier. Father Gallitzin was probably sent to the Livingston family because they were of Pennsylvania German extraction and he spoke that language fluently. The priest remained with the family for three months, and during that time, he recorded a great many strange events. At the end of his three months of observation, he recommended that the family receive an exorcism. In fact, he decided that he would perform it. Father Gallitzin began the rite of exorcism, and suddenly there were rumblings and rattlings, as if a great many phantom wagons were going through the house. The priest was so unnerved by the phantom sounds that he was unable to complete the exorcism. He then contacted Father Cahill and asked him to return to do the exorcism.

Father Cahill returned to the Livingston home to perform the exorcism. He commanded the evil spirits to leave the family and harm no one. For hours, the good Father did battle against the stubborn entity, but at last the spirit fled. Before Father Cahill left the Livingston home, he also performed a full Mass.

The Livingstons subsequently converted to Catholicism, and eventually they deeded more than thirty-four acres of their farm to the Catholic Church. This plot was called Priest Field and supposedly was given in gratitude for the help that the Catholic Church had given the Livingston family.

In a strange footnote to the events, a mysterious stranger appeared at the Livingston farm one day the following winter. The family took in the stranger and offered him warm clothes and shoes. They fed and housed him for three days, during which time he repaid their kindnesses by teaching them about Catholicism. The man told them that where he came from, it was never cold or hot. Livingston asked him where that could possibly be, and the stranger said cryptically, "From my Father's house."

On the third day, the stranger told the family that he must leave. Livingston and his family begged the stranger to stay and instruct them further, but he told them that his time had come and he could not stay any longer. As he stepped through the gate to leave the farm, he simply disappeared before the eyes of the astonished family. It was in that one moment that they began to believe that they had been sent an angel to teach them the way to Heaven.

Although officially the haunting ended with a Catholic Mass, strange phenomena did continue around the Livingston home. It was reported that disembodied voices instructed them in the rosary and phantom arms appeared to teach them how to make a cross in the air.

The spirit known as Wizard's Clip is one of the most well-documented poltergeists in history. There is no doubt that something otherworldly occurred on Adam Livingston's farm, and that this spirit seemed bent upon directing this good Lutheran man in another spiritual direction. There is no doubt that the Adam Livingston family lived through one of America's most significant hauntings.

Berkeley Castle

Sitting perched on Warm Spring Mountain above the quiet spa town of Berkeley Springs is a large, gray stone castle that would look more at home in medieval Europe. But Berkeley Castle is a unique part of the history of this old town. The story of Berkeley Castle has nothing to do with the town's Colonial roots. Instead, the castle sprang from a great love story. Maryland businessman Colonel Samuel Suit built Berkeley Castle for his young bride in 1885. The castle was a wedding gift and also the culmination of a strange romantic courtship.

Colonel Suit was a forty-one-year-old businessman who had fought in the Civil War under Robert E. Lee. During Reconstruction, he held the position of minister to England in the administrations of Presidents Grant and Hayes. It was a high compliment for a Southern colonel to be so trusted by two former Northern generals.

One evening, Colonel Suit was in Berkeley Springs to take the water and attend a lavish annual ball, when he spotted a young girl dancing across the room. She was the most exquisite creature he had ever seen, but she was only seventeen years old. Still, his heart beat faster when he looked at her, so he inquired about her. She was Martha Rosa Pelham, the daughter of wealthy Alabama Congressman Charles Pelham.

Colonel Suit sought to make the acquaintance of the young girl and danced with her that night. Young Rosa realized that she had won the man's affection, but she was far too young for a serious relationship. Colonel Suit asked Rosa to marry him that night, but she refused.

The following year, Colonel Suit returned to Berkeley Springs to attend the annual ball and see the young woman who had stolen his heart. This time, he arranged to sit at Rosa Pelham's table and spoke with the young woman at length. He requested the privilege of several dances, and by the end of the night, the Colonel was so smitten that he proposed marriage to the young woman a second time. She simply laughed at his proposal, and Colonel Suit had to return home to pine away for the young girl.

For five years, the Colonel waited for young Rosa. The two kept in contact throughout that time, and in 1883 Colonel Suit found out that Rosa would be in Berkeley Springs. He decided to make another trip to Berkeley Springs as well. By now the twenty-two-year-old woman was also intrigued with the older man who pursued her so ardently. Once again the Colonel arranged to be seated near Rosa at a dinner party. During the evening, the conversation turned to castles, and Rosa said that she had always dreamed of living in one. Colonel Suit took a piece of paper from his pocket. He drew a picture of Berkeley Castle in Bath, England, and slid it across the table to Rosa. She took the paper, glanced at it, and looked at the Colonel questioningly.

"If you marry me," he said, "I will build you this castle for your home."

Supposedly, young Rosa slid the paper back across the table to the Colonel and said, "If you build me this castle, I will marry you."

Only three days after Colonel Suit's proposal, he and Rosa were married in Washington, D.C.

So Colonel Samuel Suit, now forty-six years old, purchased the land above the spa at Berkeley Springs and began construction on the castle. He spent nearly $100,000 on the castle. But May-December romances do not often end happily.

The Colonel called his half-size castle his "cottage." He and Rosa took up residence in the partially completed castle three years later. In 1888, months before the castle was finished, Colonel Suit died. Rosa insisted that the castle be completed, and she decided to remain there with her three small children.

When the Colonel died, the local gossips began talking in Berkeley Springs, and people speculated that perhaps Rosa had poisoned her husband. People said it was quite suspicious that Colonel Suit had died soon after changing his will to leave everything to his beloved Rosa. Eventually those rumors died down, as Rosa gave the local gossips much more to talk about.

The young widow loved to throw parties at the castle, and her parties were more lavish than any that Berkeley Springs had ever seen. She would hire a train to pick up her friends throughout the country, and then she would throw elaborate house parties that would last for weeks. The people of Berkeley Springs not only learned to tolerate her parties, but began to anticipate them as well. She often booked entire hotels for her guests to stay at, so the town of Berkeley Springs profited from Rose's extravagances. She also threw a lavish party once a year on the grounds of the Berkeley Springs spa for the townspeople. It was her way of showing them her appreciation. She also showed many acts of charity to local people and became well known as a woman with a kind heart.

Rosa was still a beautiful young woman, and soon men began to show an interest in her. She had several suitors over the years, but she never again married. There was a clause in the will that stated that if she remarried, she would lose everything her husband had bequeathed her. According to some local sources, Rosa's parties were actually excuses for her to meet men. Some people claim that she would invite large groups of people to her parties so that she could meet specific men. It was said that she would attend the party only long enough to dance one dance, and then she would leave with one of her suitors.

The young woman also enjoyed the dramatic. Any guest lucky enough to stay within the castle walls would be treated to an evening of fortune-telling by the local gypsies that Rosa would hire. Her most intimate associates were also invited to join the gambling that she held in the drawing room that had once housed her husband's office.

Local lore has it that she nicknamed one of her suitors Jawbone, and that he often attended the gambling parties. It is said that one night, Jawbone and Rosa had a heated disagreement. The couple left the party still fighting. They ended up arguing viciously on the roof of the castle, where Rosa often held parties. Rosa later said that Jawbone grabbed her, and she pushed him back as she struggled to get away. One way or another, Jawbone fell over the battlements to his death from the castle roof. There are stories that claim that he haunted Rosa for the rest of her life.

A second lover of Rosa's also died within the castle walls. It is said that Rosa and her lover were arguing as they walked down the grand staircase in the castle. He grabbed her and they struggled on the staircase. Rosa reached out to swat or push him with the point of her parasol, and the man lost his balance. He fell from near the top of the stairs down to the bottom, where he lay without moving. Rosa's second lover died almost instantly.

Rosa's only daughter died as teenager on the property. Her body was buried near the castle. In recent years, a caretaker found what looked like a tombstone in the high weeds as he was clearing away brush from around the castle walls. He knew the story about Rosa's daughter and wondered whether this lonely grave was that of the teenage girl.

Colonel Suit had never intended for Rosa to squander his fortune so carelessly, and eventually the money ran out. Rosa was forced to move to a small farmhouse near the castle when creditors took the building and contents to pay off a $4,000 debt. She lived in abject poverty for several years and was forced to try to make a living by raising chickens and making jelly and preserves for sale. Eventually Rosa's son came back from where he was living out west and took his mother home with him. Rosa died penniless and far from the castle she loved so well.

Through the years, the castle went through several incarnations. A gentleman named Walter Royal from England purchased the castle. It was Walter who restored the castle to much of its original grandeur. He obtained several pieces of furniture that had belonged to the Suits and filled the castle with priceless antiques.

The castle later served other purposes. It was a private home, it housed a dinner theater, and it has now become a home again. Perhaps the strangest period in the castle's history was when it was purchased by the Berkeley Castle Paranormal Research Center and run by Joe Holbert and a group of twenty investors. This group was drawn to the castle because it is the only Norman-style castle in North America and because it is thought to have a lot of paranormal history. They hoped that the twelve-room castle might draw paranormal enthusiasts from around the world, but they wound up selling the castle shortly after they began the project.

There seems little doubt that the castle and the grounds are indeed haunted. Both residents of the castle and tour guides have reported that Rosa has returned. Guests have reported seeing a woman looking out one of the tower windows in Rosa's bedroom. Rosa spent many hours by the windows looking out at the town of Berkeley Springs and the castle grounds.

The drawing room is believed to be one of the more haunted rooms, and here folks claim to hear the clink of crystal and the sound of laughter. Some people have reported capturing a ghostly man in photographs in that room. The drawing room was Colonel Suit's old office, and it still houses one of the rare pieces that actually belonged to the Suit family. In 1993, staff at the castle witnessed an amazing event. While they watched, a quill pen lying on the antique writing desk rose into the air and whirled around for several seconds. The amazed staff members fled and were quick to say that they had never felt comfortable in that room.

Through the years, many staff members and caretakers have said they heard heavy thumps on the second floor and the sound of something being dragged across the floor. One former caretaker reported often hearing what sounded like a heavy chest being dragged through the drawing room. When he looked into the room to see if everything was okay, he found nothing out of place.

The groundskeepers have heard the sounds of a party being held on the rooftop, complete with laughter and the tinkling of glass. They have also heard the scream of someone falling from the rooftop and the sound of a heavy object thudding against the ground, followed by the sound of someone dragging something heavy away from the castle wall.

The sound of children playing has been heard in the dining room when there are no children in the building, and guests have reported hearing their names being called while they were alone in the castle. Some folks also claim to have seen people on the walls of the stairwell. Once a big mirror was rehung upside down by accident, and a woman kept appearing in it and startling people until someone realized that the mirror was upside down and had it put right. Employees have reported being locked into rooms in the house. The doors would not open despite their best efforts, but someone from the outside could open the door to release the person trapped inside.

A former caretaker related a most interesting and unusual tale about the castle that has never been reported publicly before. On several occasions, while alone on late summer evenings, he was roused from his work by what sounded like a large cat screaming in terror. At first he thought there were mountain lions outside the castle, but he found no sign of them. The man also did volunteer work at the local historical society, where he found an interesting article that possibly explained the sounds of the phantom big cat on the castle property. During Rosa Suit's tenure as owner of the castle, it is said, she often allowed the traveling carnivals and circuses to park along the edge of her property. She occasionally employed the gypsy fortune-tellers to entertain her guests, and she was often friendlier with the traveling shows than the local farmers were. While one traveling circus was parked on her property, a terrible fire broke out in the animal wagons. Several wagons caught fire, but only one was completely destroyed—the tiger cage. The tiger cages were in the center of the lineup and appear to have been where the fire started. Most of the animals were saved from the flames, but there was no way to rescue the poor doomed cats, and they burned alive in the conflagration. Witnesses described the terrible screams of the cats as the fire consumed them. The caretaker could not help but think of the horrible cat screams he had heard only weeks before. He wondered whether on the anniversary of their death, the big cats relived their final horrible moments on earth.

At one time, Berkeley Castle was a favored spot for weddings. The castle was prone to power failures during the wedding ceremonies, but not one power outage was ever reported during the receptions. Perhaps Rosa was trying to hurry the marriage along so that the old castle could once again be filled with the sounds of a party.

Today the castle is once again owned privately, and stories of the specters of Samuel and Rosa are no longer circulated. But if they are still in their castle, then they are enjoying this most unique treasure that they gave to Berkeley Springs.

The Curse of Berkeley Springs

History and folklore often merge over the years, and it can become difficult to know how to unravel the two. The curse of Berkeley Springs is one such story. It came from a historian and folklore collector in the Berkeley Springs area who spent many years collecting the little-known tales of Morgan County.

The town of Berkeley Springs is a charming little tourist town where a person can rest, relax, and simply enjoy the peace of the spa. The warm waters bubble up into little stone pools and through a race stream where every sunny day finds children playing and adults soaking their feet. Private baths within the spa can be rented for those who seriously want to take the waters. Drinking the water is also recommended. The mineral waters contain nitrates and sulfates that are helpful to the human body. The springs remain at a constant 74 degrees coming up from the earth and produce two thousand gallons of water a minute.

Taking the waters is an old tradition at Berkeley Springs. A small stone pool bears a sign saying it is George Washington's bathing tub, and this is not a phony gimmick, as Washington often took the waters of Berkeley Springs. He first came to Berkeley Springs, or Bath, as it was then called, in 1747 as a sixteen-year-old surveyor. He enjoyed his visit and quickly came to believe that there was much potential for profit within the settlement. Throughout his life, Washington did a great deal of land speculation, and he was quick to explore the potential for the area. He eventually came to own property in Berkeley Springs.

The first settler to the area built a cabin in 1745, and when young George Washington first visited the town, it was filled with people who had come for the waters. Wealthy people arrived in covered wagons and brought along their servants. Others camped near the springs. The area was an open sandy pit lined with rocks to create a sort of bowl where the water could be reached easily. The ill and infirm, the wealthy who could afford to quest for better health, and those desperate for whatever relief they could find all were drawn here.

The town was listed in George Washington's private journal as "Ye Springs of Ye Town of Bath." Taking the waters was all the rage in England and Europe. The old Roman baths in England had been found and refurbished only a little while before, and taking the water in the Roman baths was a popular pastime in the mother country. The town in England where the Roman baths were located was called Bath. Berkeley Springs has the distinction of having two names simultaneously. The city is still officially Bath, but the post office was given the name of Berkeley Springs. Thus people pass the post office of Berkeley Springs as they enter the city of Bath. The confusion about the name, however, never seemed to hurt the town's reputation.

The springs were old when Lord Fairfax and George Washington first dipped their toes in the warm water. The local native tribes knew all about the springs. They had long bathed in them both for better health and for pleasure. The Indians who had used the springs for thousands of years first told the whites of the water's health benefits. The springs were attributed with healing illnesses, skin problems, and much more.

There is little doubt that George Washington was enchanted with the warm-water springs. Washington and a group of family and friends formed the town of Bath, and the town was issued a charter in 1776. He obtained ownership of the land and began to shape his dream. In 1802, a hotel was listed as being operated by John Hunter "at the sign of George Washington." Many of the founding fathers and other prominent men began to frequent the springs at Bath.

In 1842, Strother House built a building that would later become the Berkeley Springs Hotel. Baths were officially separated for men and women so that they could all partake of the waters. The most fashionable citizens in the New World paid to go there but before all of this occurred, a curse was supposedly placed on the land.

Lord Fairfax had recognized early on that the springs were going to be commercially useful, but there was an obstacle to the grand plan for fine hotels and bathing pools. The natives and poor whites that had settled in the area were already using the warm-water springs. Lord Fairfax realized that the wealthy would not want to dip in the same water where commoners and heathens were. Furthermore, the natives represented potential danger, so he had to have them driven out. Supposedly he posted men at the warm springs to drive off anyone who came to use them without his permission. The whites were fairly easy to drive off. They didn't want trouble from Lord Fairfax, who was governor of the region. He could make life easy or hard for them and could take their lands if they annoyed him. So they quickly gave up bathing in the waters of Bath.

But discouraging the Indians was not so simple. For longer than anyone could remember, these people had used the warm springs. They believed that they had a right to do so, and they continued to sneak the use of the waters. At first they were simply ordered away, but that did not work. Next they were beaten when caught, but that did not work either. They truly did not understand why anyone would deny them the right to use a healing place that the Great Spirit had given to them all.

As time went by, Lord Fairfax grew angry about the belligerence of the natives who would not obey him. He finally ordered that deadly force should be used against the next native caught bathing in the springs.

The next native turned out to be an elderly medicine man who probably was using the warm mineral waters to ease arthritis or other illnesses. The man was shot when he refused to leave the springs. While the old man lay on the ground bleeding to death, he demanded to know why he had been shot. One of Lord Fairfax's men leaned over the old man and said, "You were shot because you would not leave the springs alone. Lord Fairfax said to drive you all off so that he can build his hotel here."

Though the old medicine man spoke a little English, he did not know what the word "hotel" meant, but he did understand that he had been shot because of it. It is said that he cursed the land that would later be called Berkeley Springs, saying that every hotel built there would be destroyed by fire. With the curse on his lips, the poor old man died.

After that Lord Fairfax got his wish, and the natives no longer used the springs. They mourned the loss of their medicine man and understood that his fate would be their fate too if they did not stay away from the waters.

But perhaps the old medicine man's curse took, because Berkeley Springs has more than a passing history of hotels burning down. The great Berkeley Springs Spa burned down. The Park View Hotel or Inn was also destroyed by fire. Other hotels within the town have succumbed to a blaze as well. Today there are motels, bed-and-breakfasts, spas, and inns in Berkeley Springs, but not a single hotel is found in the town.

Is the lack of hotels merely an oversight on the part of the building owners, or have they learned that calling their business a hotel ensures a fiery future for their venture? Though fire was an ever-present threat in Colonial America, and many buildings did burn down, Berkeley Springs does seem to have had more than its share of hotels go up in flames.

Potomac Highlands

The Ghost Light of Cole Mountain

Looming above the small village of Moorefield is Cole Mountain. It is part of the Appalachian Mountain range and is much like the other mountains in this range. But there is something about Cole Mountain that makes it very different—it is home to a ghost light. People usually claim that the light is reddish and moves rapidly across the mountain before them. This Ghost Light exhibits behavior that makes it different from any other ghost light in America. It has been known to approach people, and it makes an unearthly screaming sound on occasion that frightens folks away from the land it seems to protect. The light was first sighted in the early 1800s and is reported to this day.

A story often told in Moorefield might explain the origins of this strange light. Wealthy landowner Charles Jones was an elderly man who lived near the town. The gentleman owned several slaves, but he was known to be particularly fond of one particular young slave man whom he often took hunting with him. Jones enjoyed hunting and training his pack of dogs at night. The young slave often accompanied his master and carried the lantern so that his master could see.

One night the two men were running the dogs as usual. The young slave carried the lantern high and ran ahead after the dogs so that Jones could make his way. Suddenly the dogs began to bay loudly as if they had treed a raccoon, and Jones instructed the slave to hurry ahead. When the slave turned around, he found that he was alone and called out to his master. But Jones did not respond. The slave turned back to search for his master. He was very fond of the old man because the man treated him kindly, and he was frightened for him.

By dawn, the slave realized he had to go for help and returned to the house. With trepidation, he told the family about how Jones had simply disappeared the night before. Had anyone else told them this strange tale, the family might have accused them of harming the old man, but everyone knew that this lad was particularly fond of him.

The family began a manhunt that lasted all day and well into the night. Without rest, the slave returned to the woods to show the searchers where he had last seen the old man. He stayed with them all day and most of the night as they hunted for any clue as to the fate of Mr. Jones.

The disappearance of the wealthy landowner caused quite a stir in the community. For days, the authorities and volunteers searched for him, but at last they had to give up. The only one reluctant to end the search was the slave, who seemed to feel responsible for the old man and continued looking every time he had a chance.

Life went on, and the family learned to accept the fact that the old man was gone. But on the one-year anniversary of the disappearance of Charles Jones, the story took a new twist. That night, the slave decided to take a lantern and return to the woods to look for his master one more time. What he thought he might find, no one would ever know, because this time the slave disappeared.

Shortly after the slave's disappearance, people began to claim that they saw a red light floating along the side of Cole Mountain. It did not take long for the locals to associate the red light with the missing slave. They began to say that the same fate had befallen the slave as had befallen his master. People said that both men were dead, and that in death the slave was still looking for the old man.

Since then, many people have had encounters with the ghost light of Cole Mountain. What makes the light unique is that it seems to seek out hunters in particular to show itself to. Years ago, a group of raccoon hunters claimed to have encountered the ghost light. They said that it slowly approached them, and as it drew close, it suddenly emitted a loud scream that frightened them so badly that they ran off. One of the men got off three shots at the ghost light before he followed his comrades. The light seemed to chase them down a hillside before it suddenly went out at the bottom of the hill.

To this day, no one has ever found any clue as to what happened to Charles Jones or his slave. That mystery has yet to be solved, as does the mystery of the ghost light. Engineers have tried to explain away the phenomenon as car lights, but cars were not driving the roads when the light was first spotted. Others have talked about light refractions and other quasiscientific explanations, but these theories cannot explain every sighting. Thus the mysteries of the two men and the Cole Mountain ghost light remain part of the lore of the mountains of West Virginia.

The Headless Ghost of George Van Meter

Near present-day Petersburg is a little hollow known locally as Dorcas Hollow. It's the type of place that normally would go unnoticed, but it has earned a reputation that has kept the name of the little hollow and the man who died there alive for nearly two hundred years.

George Van Meter came to America to begin a new life. He had been a carpenter in Germany, but in America he and his family worked their little farm, and George picked up whatever carpentry work he could. He had chosen to settle in a remote part of what was then the frontier of Virginia. In fact, there were only fifteen families in the whole county where George lived.

George and his family did not mind the isolation, but it was dangerous to live so far from the protection of a fort. Indian attacks were a very real threat, and the only hope of survival was for the locals to band together at the local fort. George, however, had settled far away from the nearest fort.

On July 4, George and his son David were working in the fields not far from the little cabin that they had built. They felt uneasy as they worked in the hot sun. They were all too aware that the Huron Indians had raided and burned other farms nearby in the previous weeks. George would be glad when they could return to the cabin and wash up so that they could go to town to take part in the festivities planned for the evening. But work had to come before pleasure, so the two bent their backs to the burdens at hand.

George had just sat down beneath a tree to rest when he saw a sight that made his blood freeze. A small band of Huron Indians had just come running out of the woods near where they had been working. Quickly George grabbed up his son and ordered the boy to go back and get his family. George charged David with leading his mother and siblings to safety at the fort while he held off the Indians long enough for the boy to get the family to safety.

David rushed home and, with the help of his mother, hurried the children to the fort. Once there, he told his tale of seeing the Huron Indians and how his father was holding them off. Several men from the fort grabbed up weapons and hurried back to rescue George if it wasn't too late. David accompanied the men in the rescue party, but as they neared the farm, they saw that the cabin was burning. The only parts that remained were the chimneys at either end of the structure.

In the fields, they found the mutilated corpse of George Van Meter. His body was so disfigured that it was hard to recognize as human. The men quickly ascertained that George's head had been cut off. They sent David back to the fort and began a search for the missing head. The men looked until after darkness fell. The head was simply gone, and they speculated that the Huron had carted it off as a grisly trophy. The men feared that the Huron would attack the settlement while they were gone and decided that they could not waste any more time looking for Van Meter's head.

To the relief of all, the Indians never attacked in town. The following morning, however, a little boy found a cooking pot on the steps to the meetinghouse. He opened the lid on the pot and let out a horrible cry. George Van Meter's boiled head was staring up at him. The Huron had sneaked in during the night and left the pot to terrify and unnerve the settlers.

Shortly after Van Meter's murder, people began to drift back into Dorcas Hollow. Soon stories began to circulate that folks were seeing the headless specter of George Van Meter walking around his burned-out homestead. It was speculated that Van Meter was looking for his head despite the fact that the boiled head and pot had been buried with him. The horror of the death of George Van Meter has echoed down through the years, and there are whispers that his spirit is still looking for what it lost so long ago.

The Spirits of Droop Mountain

Droop Mountain has earned a place in West Virginia history as the site of the largest Civil War battle ever fought in the state. The battle occurred on November 6, 1863. General William Averell was trying to drive the Confederate forces out of the Greenbrier territory when his four thousand Union troops met seventeen hundred Confederate soldiers commanded by General John Echols. Echols positioned his soldiers on the high ground, where they put up a valiant fight. In the end, there were nearly four hundred casualties, and many of the dead were left unburied across the mountain. The small cemetery behind the state park office today is officially said to be the site where the dead were buried, but it is common knowledge that many men were laid to rest in unmarked graves across the hills of Droop Mountain.

The first ghost story associated with Droop Mountain took place about two years after the battle. One afternoon in 1865, Nancy and Betty Snedegar, two little girls who lived in the area along the west side of Droop Mountain, were sent to the eastern slope of the mountain to pick berries. While they were there, the children stumbled upon two old muskets abandoned during the battle. The girls picked up their deadly find and were startled when stones started flying at them. They quickly looked around but did not see who was throwing the stones. The children grabbed up their gruesome prize and their berry pails and hurried home.

By all accounts, what occurred at the Snedegar home was classic poltergeist activity. The girls were sent out to do the evening milking and suddenly found themselves being pelted with stones and sticks. They were shocked when the stones and sticks actually seemed to penetrate through the walls of the barn to strike them. They ran back to the house and the safety of their parents, but whatever unseen force was after them seemed to follow them. Stones and sticks passed unimpeded through the cabin walls and flew down the chimney, knocking the lid from the cooking pot on the fire. The sheepskin rugs on the floor suddenly seemed to come alive and stood up on end. The andirons that held logs in the fireplace jumped out of place and slid across the room. Mrs. Snedegar's brother was pelted with stones when he attempted to visit the family.

The little girls gathered up the stones in the house and took them to a sinkhole nearby, where they began to throw them in. To their amazement, the stones flew back out of the hole and pelted the children until they ran away. At last the two muskets were taken back to the old battlefield where the children had found them, and the haunting ceased as quickly as it had begun.

Throughout the years, there have been some recurring ghostly sightings on the mountainside. A replica cannon is on display at the park, and several people have claimed to see a Confederate soldier sitting on it and smoking a cigarette on early fall evenings. Other people talk about seeing a headless Confederate specter near Spring Creek Mountain. The first known sighting of the headless soldier was when Edgar Walton and a friend encountered the headless soldier late one evening. Fifty years later, Walton's two daughters and one son-in-law also saw the headless apparition. They were cutting wood late one fall afternoon near where their father had his encounter when they heard a low moaning sound. The trio looked up and saw the headless Confederate spirit pass them by.

A ghostly infantry regiment is also said to march across the mountain. On numerous occasions, people have claimed to see soldiers marching along in formation, the men carrying their muskets as they march into battle. A phantom cavalry troop has also been seen riding across the mountain, with an officer mounted on a white horse leading the soldiers. The men had on blue jackets and khaki-colored pants and carried saddlebags similar to those used by the U.S. Cavalry. Sometimes the phantom cavalry troop is not seen but only heard. There are stories of people who have heard horses riding down on them hard but could not see anything coming their way. Throughout the years, several people have reported this frightening ghostly phenomenon.

Even some of the homes on Droop Mountain are said to be haunted. In his book *Last Sleep: The Battle of Droop Mountain, November 6, 1863*, Terry Lowry includes the story of one family that believes that their home might be haunted by one of the dead soldiers. Although this property is not on what is considered part of the battlefield, they have found minie balls throughout the property and believe that a skirmish took place on the grounds. The people even have reported capturing someone looking out of a window in their home as they took a photograph when the house was supposed to be empty.

Some of the superintendents in charge of Droop Mountain State Park have had their own stories to tell. The superintendent's home and grounds apparently are also home to several apparitions. One superintendent reported hearing strange screams in the cranberry bog near his home. He thought that an animal might be trapped in the bog, but he could find nothing when he searched it. Another superintendent's small daughter was frightened by a Confederate soldier that she saw lying in their yard. The child went to find her mother, but when the two returned, the phantom had disappeared. This child saw the ghostly figure long before reenactors were popular at the park.

In the 1930s, the Civilian Conservation Corps (CCC) built Camp Price on Droop Mountain. Some of the 220 young men and boys who worked at the camp had occasion to report ghostly events. The sound of marching was heard outside of the cabins, but the young men could find no one outside when they went to investigate. When some of them tried to sneak back into camp after visiting the town nearby late at night, they said they were challenged by disembodied cries of "Who goes there?" Perhaps the young men were victims of pranks, but considering the other accounts of the hauntings of Droop Mountain, they very well may have had their own ghostly encounters.

Droop Mountain also seems to be haunted by a phantom horse. A ghostly dappled gray horse has been seen standing in the mists on the mountain early in the morning and late at night. The horse seems to be poised as if waiting for a command from his invisible rider, and then it simply is gone. Is this horse the long-dead mount of some unfortunate cavalry officer? Perhaps the horse, like the ghostly soldiers, is playing his part in the eternal battle the spirits are still fighting on Droop Mountain.

The beauty and solitude of Droop Mountain make the area feel peaceful, and the idea of ghosts here seems silly. But late in the evening when the mist rolls in, there is a change in the air along the mountaintop, and it is no longer difficult to believe that ghosts stalk the night.

The Darkish Knob

When slavery was the rule of the land, a hill outside of Parsons earned a terrible reputation. The hill was known locally as the Darkish Knob, and it looked like virtually every other hill in the area, but local folks knew that there was something distinctly sinister about that knob. Many of the residents of Parsons believed that the Darkish Knob was haunted.

One of the many paths of the Underground Railroad ran through the Parsons area and around the Darkish Knob. Fleeing slaves had to skirt the dangerous hill covered with loose shale to get to a house hidden at its base, where they would find safety.

Often slaveholders hired slavecatchers to track down runaway slaves. The slavecatchers worked very much like bounty hunters do today. They received a list of names of the escaped slaves, the amount of bounty on each one, and any other information that might help them in their search. Then they would begin their hunt. Often they checked nearby trails where slaves had been captured before. This forced the slaves to seek new and even more treacherous routes to freedom. One route that was favored by slaves was over the mountains of West Virginia, but traveling at night through the deep piney woods and over the loose rocky slopes was dangerous.

At the base of the Darkish Knob was a small house where shelter and food awaited the weary slave. The house was so well hidden, however, that at night it was difficult to locate. One night, a young black woman was hurrying on horseback toward the shelter of this house when she realized that the slavecatchers were on her trail. In her haste, she missed the house and continued up over the steep knob. The terrified girl panicked and kicked the horse's flank to hurry it along. She was suddenly plunged into a desperate chase for her very life.

The night was inky black, and she could barely see what was ahead of her. The horse ran on blindly, urged by the girl's heels in his flanks and by the fear he sensed from his mistress. The thundering hooves of the slavecatchers' horses only accentuated the need for the horse to run. The girl navigated the knob to the best of her ability, but in her panic, she blundered up the knob at full speed. The horse tried to hold its footing on the slippery hillside, and he finally made it to the top. The girl turned back to look at the slavecatchers before she spurred the horse forward down the other side of the Darkish Knob. The horse slipped on the sliding shale as he tried to traverse down the hillside, and they both plunged to their death.

Over the years since, many people have claimed to hear terrible screams coming from the Darkish Knob around the anniversary of the girl's death. The screams are the cries of a young woman in terror, but no one has ever found any rational reason for them. If the young woman is reliving her death, then one can only feel sorrow for her and the fact that she is caught in an eternal struggle for freedom.

Bibliography

Books

Cohen, Daniel. *Railway Ghosts and Highway Horrors.* Scholastic Books, 1991.

Coleman, Christopher K. *Dixie Spirits.* Cumberland House, 2002.

Dougherty, Shirley. *A Ghostly Tour of Harpers Ferry.* EIGMID Publishing Company, 1982.

Gavenda, Walter, and Michael T. Shoemaker. *A Guide to Haunted West Virginia.* Peter's Creek Publishing, 2001.

Guiley, Rosemary Ellen. *The Encyclopedia of Ghosts and Spirits.* Facts on File, 1992.

Hall, Mark A. *Thunderbirds: America's Living Legends of Giant Birds.* Paraview Press, 2004.

Hauck, Dennis William. *Haunted Places.* Penguin Books, 1994.

Horn, Sallie C. *A History of the Town of Bath (Berkeley Springs, W.Va.).* Morgan County Historical and Genealogical Society, 2003.

Lowry, Terry. *Last Sleep: The Battle of Droop Mountain, November 6,1863.*

Musick, Ruth Ann. *Coffin Hollow and Other Ghost Tales.* University of Kentucky Press, 1977.

———. *The Telltale Lilac Bush and Other West Virginia Ghost Tales.* University of Kentucky Press, 1965.

Nelson, Scott Reynolds. *Steel Drivin' Man: John Henry, the Untold Story of an American Legend.* Oxford University Press, 2006.

Norman, Michael, and Beth Scott. *Haunted America.* Tor Books, Tom Doherty Associates, 1994.

———. *Historic Haunted America.* Tor Books, Tom Doherty Associates, 1995.

Peck, Catherine. *QPB Treasury of North American Folktales.* Philip Lief Group, 1998.

Reevy, Tony. *Ghost Train! American Railroad Ghost Legends.* TLC Publishing, 1998.

Bibliography

Roberts, Nancy. *America's Most Haunted Places.* Sandlapper Publishing Co., 1974.

———. *Civil War Ghost Stories and Legends.* University of South Carolina Press, 1992.

Rule, Leslie. *Ghosts Among Us.* Andrews McMeel Publishing, 2004.

Samples, Mack. *The Devil's Tea Tables.* Quarrier Press, 2005.

———. *Elk River Ghosts Tales and Lore.* Quarrier Press, 2002.

Sheppard, Susan. *Cry of the Banshee.* Whitechapel Productions Press, 2004.

Taylor, Troy. *Down in the Darkness.* Whitechapel Productions Press, 2003.

———. *Out Past the Campfire Light.* Whitechapel Productions Press, 2004.

———. *Spirits of the Civil War.* Whitechapel Productions Press, 1999.

Web Sites

afgen.com/john_brown1.html

groups.yahoo.com/group/WVGHIS

magick.wirefire.com

wheeling.weirton.lib.wv.us/landmark/historic/monpl01.htm

www.about.com

www.berkeleysprings.com

www.boudillion.com/Moth/mothman.html

www.callwva.com/hauntings

www.dupontcastle.com/castles/berkeley.htm

www.ferrum.edu/applit/bibs/tales/JHenry.htm

www.hauntedhistory.net/moundsville.html

www.inspiredink.com/article.asp?ID = 21

www.juceenewsdaily.com/0205/haunted-west-virginia.html

www.nps.gov/hafe

www.paresearchers.com/ghosts/Ghost_expedition/moundsville_wv_2004

www.prairieghosts.com

www.shadowlands.net/places/westvirginia.htm

www.stratalum.org/august1/newby.htm

www.tonyabolden.com/bkstrongmen.html

www.tonyabolden.com/excstrngmen.html

www.tourpikecounty.com

www.wesclark.com/jw/newby.html

www.westvirginiaghosthunters.com

www.wikipedia.com

www.wm.edu/news/indix.php?id = 6082

www.wvghosts.com

www.wvpentours.com

www.wvpentours.com/ghosts.htm

Acknowledgments

I WOULD LIKE TO THANK KYLE WEAVER, MY EXCEPTIONAL EDITOR AT
Stackpole Books, for his hard work and professionalism. His belief
in me has meant a lot. Thanks to Amy Cooper, associate editor, for
her help and patience as we worked on this project. Heather Adel
Wiggins created the eerie artwork that made the book fly.

Writing a book is never a solo task and many people deserve
mention and thanks. Mark Nesbitt, my colleague and my friend,
whose faith and friendship have blessed me more than he will ever
know. His wife Carol, whose long-suffering patience as we tell our
tales is much appreciated. (Scott owes you a drink!)

I thank my friends who have worked tirelessly to help me
research the stories within this volume. Adam opened his home,
heart, and family history to me—and so did Jenifer and Ashley
Roberts. Larry Phelps scouted out tales and Jenifer Roberts spent
countless hours teaching me about the ghosts of the great state of
West Virginia.

Scott Crownover has been my friend, cheerleader, and greatest
critic, and I thank him for being all of those things. His patience
and sympathetic ear has often helped me find my way as I worked
on this book.

My mother taught me to be strong, persevere, and always have
faith. Her quiet support has stood me well. She has always been
my rock.

My brother Terry and my sister Georgette shared my first adventures with me, and we had great laughs in haunted houses when

Acknowledgments

we should have been scared. I will always treasure our adventures and the simple joy of a good, scary story with them. Andy and Jerry have always been there when I needed them and that is priceless.

I want to send my thanks to the folks at the Ghost Research Foundation, whom I have grown to love. To Linda, Charley, Patty, and many others, I send my humble appreciation. They have shared my dreams and have made them come true.

My sons Daniel, Michael, and Ben are always my inspiration. They have patiently waited while I worked, listened to my tales, and loved me through it all. God placed them on this planet to remind me that I am truly blessed. They have been patient when I couldn't play. Now you may collect on the hikes, the picnics, and the baked cookies that I couldn't deliver on while I worked. Oh, and no more take-out—real meals now, because the book is done!

About the Author

PATTY A. WILSON LIVES IN CENTRAL PENNSYLVANIA AND HAS BEEN A writer and historian for more than 20 years. She is the author of *The Pennsylvania Ghost Guide* and *Where Dead Men Walk* and coauthor of *Boos & Brews* with Scott Crownover and *Haunted Pennsylvania* with Mark Nesbitt. Patty cofounded the Ghost Research Foundation, which was the first field research group to teach at the Rhine Research Center in Durham, North Carolina, and Lily Dale Assembly in New York.